Angels of the Odd

JAMES WARRENDER

Copyright © 2014 James Warrender

All rights reserved.

ISBN-10 1492803049
ISBN-13 978-1492803041

www.jameswarrender.webs.com
james.warrender@mail.com

For Lesley and Connor
Thank you for being my friends

CONTENTS

Acknowledgments	i
Introduction	1
Explaining The Unexplained	17
Famous Ghosts & Their Hunters	131
Hunting The Unknown	223
Haunted Sites	257
Conclusion	321

ACKNOWLEDGMENTS

I would like to take time to thank a few people for their help.

First off to my fantastic family and friends for their continued support. My extended family at Tutbury Castle including Lesley, Gareth, Debbie and Judith. Emma Bragginton and Jennifer Nicoll for taking time to proof read the book and for their friendship. Graeme Milne for inspiring me to write this book. All those managers, night watch men and women and locations that have allowed me to investigate their property. Ken Mackintosh and Loraine Findlay for the help, support and friendship in getting this far in my paranormal career. Finally, to my friends at ESP Paranormal: Ian, Claire, Jonathon, Neil and Anne. Long may our investigations continue!

INTRODUCTION

I was standing in the Great Hall of Tutbury Castle. I couldn't believe it. It was the location that had first got me interested in the paranormal eight years before and now I was there. I recognised the suit of armour standing by the throne. I recognised the towers, the ruins, the chapel and the eerie staircases. It was my first time there but part of me felt like I had come home. I stood in the middle of the Great Hall looking around me, wondering how I managed to end up there.

In 2003 I was in my second year at School. Even the sound of the words "ghost" or "haunted" would give me nightmares. I can't say I was very pleased when I found out that "Life After Death" was a topic that we would cover in a Religious Education class in School. The only knowledge I had of the paranormal up until that time was overhearing some members of my family discussing visiting a psychic after a member of my family had died. Needless to say the thought of someone having the ability to talk to the dead scared me to death. I spoke to my Religious Education teacher Ken Mackintosh about what I knew. I even told him some of the ghost stories my Grandma (Or Grunny as we say in Aberdeen!) told me when I was younger, but I really didn't have that many stories to tell.

We began to work on the topic. I listened to some of my classmate's ghost stories. Looking back, I'm sure many of them were made up simply to try and frighten the class. Some may have been genuine, but as you investigate ghost stories more and more you can begin to separate the ones that people really feel like they experienced to ones that are made up.

After a while we began to study Spiritualism and Mediumship, most notably the medium George Anderson who works with spirits to help families through grief. We then moved on to look at ghosts. "Was I Scared?" I hear you ask. Yes! We watched old episodes of 'Strange But True' which just added to my fear of all things dead. Then suddenly something changed. One day we began looking at the story of 'The San Pedro Haunting'. A lady is haunted by a nasty spirit in her home and has to call in parapsychologists to investigate the case. I'll take a more in depth look at this case later on the book. As scary as this case is, I can't say I was too frightened by it. I was more interested. But this was just the very start of what was to become my passion, my career and life.

Over Summer 2003 we got satellite television installed in our house. Our very first attempt at skipping through the channels was short lived when my Mum and I found a television series which focused on people ghost hunting in buildings around the country. This particular episode was from Tutbury Castle, a very frightening looking castle in Staffordshire. The first person I saw in this episode was psychic medium Derek Acorah. I watched in awe of Derek as he communicated with the long since dead residents of the Castle and it excited me when he made hits that only the Castle Curator could verify.

Later on in the programme the curator, Lesley Smith performed as Mary, Queen of Scots. It has been reported that whilst Lesley is performing as Mary, strange things happen simultaneously around the castle. Strange lights are seen and sometimes people actually report seeing Mary. As much as I was enjoying watching Derek work, seeing Lesley in the night vision green and the Mary makeup terrified me! Little did I know back then just how much that lady who scared me to death would make such an impact on my later life.

I began to watch the paranormal programme on a regular basis and when I returned to school after the Summer I began work on my third year where I had taken on Religious Education for Standard Grade. For part of the course I could work on a project on a Religious, Moral or Philosophical subject. Naturally I chose 'Life After Death' and with my new found bravery and interest in the subject I began working closely with my teachers Ken Mackintosh and Loraine Findlay on the project. I must say they were brilliant. They allowed me to head out and do surveys on the topic, visit the library and watch as many paranormal television shows as I could to build up my project. (Which is actually the inspiration behind this book!) The only down side to the project is that I couldn't really say I had any paranormal experiences that I could write about. But that was just about to change.

One evening, I was heading home from school and took a different way than usual through a park as it was quite a nice day. I was chatting with some friends when I was suddenly distracted. I looked over to my left where there was an old ruined building and standing by the door was a faded image of a hooded woman holding a baby. I looked back to my friends then back over to where the lady stood and she was gone. I didn't say a word to anyone but wrote it all down when I got home. Looking back, maybe it was a trick of the light or maybe my own brain wanting to see something so much it delivered. Either way I felt like I had seen something. I told a few friends at school the next day who laughed at me, although Mr Mackintosh seemed interested when I handed him the document I wrote on it.

My project came together and I must say it looked pretty good! I had covered ghost theories, photos and hoaxes. I seemed to have built up a reputation at school as "that Ghostbuster" especially when the library's 'Life After Death' section had almost trebled in size because I had asked for so many books to be taken in!

By this time I felt like I wanted to know more about the paranormal. But how could

I? Every book I read was by a medium, investigator or scientist. I really wanted to get out there and investigate things for myself. As chance would have it, a Scotland based team were to host an investigation into a near by castle and were keen for people to come along and take part, so I went along. I met and got to know the team and got to take part in my first full paranormal investigation. It wasn't very active but it was good fun. It gave me a taste for investigation and soon I was heading out on investigations every other weekend!

I continued to work hard reading every book on the topic I could. I was a particular fan of Doris Stokes, Derek Acorah and Mia Dolan. I began to do more investigations and took part in ghost hunts with 'Haunted Homes' which was great fun! I later began getting involved with the only ghost team in Aberdeen, *East Scotland Paranormal.* So even back then I was establishing myself in the paranormal world.

Elsewhere in School, I was doing very well in Drama, English and Media and I really wanted a career in television. I was accepted on a course in Television Production at Aberdeen College which would last from 2008 until 2010. During my time there I was allowed to make a number of productions based around my paranormal investigations. Although I don't think my classmates were too happy about having to come to spooky, haunted locations with me!!

By 2009 I had began to take part in psychic and Mediumship development circles while still investigating with groups around the country.

In January of that year I was watching the same paranormal programme that I had first seen in 2003. Tutbury Castle curator, Lesley Smith had joined the team on a permanent basis as the historian. During a Question and Answer section on the show, Lesley urged anyone keen on the paranormal to get in touch with her at the castle to discuss the subject. Although I didn't do it right away, I did manage to pluck up the courage to make contact a few weeks later during a particularly dull College lecture. I emailed Lesley about the castle, the show she was on and about the ghosts at the Tutbury. I thought that if I was lucky, I would get a reply from her PA, in about six months, but to my surprise Lesley had replied personally by the time I got home from college that day.

During our first initial emails back and forth, we discussed ghosts, television, theatre and history. We got on very well and I was very excited when she told me she was due up to Aberdeen in just a few weeks to give a lecture and if I was able to attend she would love to meet me in person. I instantly agreed and was very excited to go. I met her for the first time at Aberdeen University 22nd July 2009 and we were good friends from that day forward.

My investigations continued during the next few months and I was lucky enough to join Aberdeen's *East Scotland Paranormal* as a guest investigator a few times at the very spooky Tolbooth Museum in Aberdeen and I had my own item in *Paranormal Magazine* which went out each month.

2011 was to be a very big year for me. I was still good friends with Lesley who had come along to my Graduation party in November 2010 and she had invited me to visit her at Tutbury Castle. I had been given the flights to Birmingham for Christmas and I was due to head down in the January.

Upon my arrival at Tutbury I was close to tears because it was such an important place in my heart. It was part of the reason I was involved in the paranormal. On the evening I arrived, Lesley had to leave me at the Castle for a while. I was up for the challenge. Nothing was going to scare me... I thought. One by one, Lesley's staff left the Castle and the last person to leave said "goodbye and good luck!" Good luck I thought? Why would I need luck?

I made a cup of tea and took it to Lesley's office which was my makeshift living room for the night. I found a radio station on the internet to listen to and I was ready to relax. As it turns out, the castle had other plans for me!!

The first odd thing that happened was the sound of footsteps in the Great Hall, which was just outside the room I was in. The first time I heard them I put it down to the building settling but the second and third times I knew they were definitely there. I found my bravery and walked out into the Great Hall to have a look around. All seemed quiet. I went back into the office and sat back down. It didn't take long before I heard a woman crying from somewhere in the building. I couldn't tell you where it came from. All I can tell you is that it was in the building somewhere.

The crying frightened me more than it really should have. I was distracted for a while when a friend called me to see how I was getting on but when I finished the call things got bad. I left the office door open so I could look out to the Great Hall when I needed to. There was definite movement out there. A black shape kept catching my eye. I decided I wanted another cup of tea and went downstairs. The footsteps began again when I was in the kitchen. Like a scene from a horror movie I began to climb the stairs back into the Great Hall where I found that the lights were flickering. I didn't get long to react to the lights because a very, very loud bang filled the room from the area of the fireplace and caused the stairway to shake.

Unsure what to do, I decided to just stay calm and have a seat downstairs for a while. I had been sitting downstairs for a while when I realised that I had left my phone in the Great Hall so I ran up to get it. While I was up there I was about to walk out the door, back downstairs when a large dish on a table by the door slid about three feet along the table towards me. I decided that I had had enough and got my cup of tea and shut myself in the office.

Thankfully Lesley came back not too long after and rescued me from the castle and put me in a hotel. I was so glad of her for doing that. I wouldn't have managed to survive an entire night there myself. I was so frightened by the events at the castle that night I actually slept with the hotel room's Bible open on the bedside table that night even though I'm not religious at all. I seriously considered my future in paranormal investigation and research feeling too frightened to continue.

The light of the next day made me think a lot more rationally about the events the night before. Maybe it was just a combination of normal sounds of the building along with faulty electrics and loose floorboards. Either way it gave me something to think about.

Later that night a ghost hunt was due to take place at the castle, hosted by The Ghostfinder Paranormal Society. It was a great insight and a very good evening of investigation with quite a lot of activity happening and I am happy to say I did manage to stay in the Castle that night... with a few other people!

I returned to Tutbury during Summer 2011 to take part in a special investigation day with Derek Acorah, the man I had idolised for as long as my interest in the paranormal had existed. I still hold very fond memories of that day close to my heart.

In November 2011 I was invited back to *East Scotland Paranormal,* who had recently re-launched and now investigated under the name *ESP Paranormal Investigation Team.* We spent a very cold and spooky night together in Castle Menzies and since then we investigate all over the country whenever we can. The team: Ian, Claire, Jonathon, Neil and Anne are a great bunch and I'm blessed that I get to investigate with them and get to call them my friends.

Ever since I began researching the paranormal in 2003 I have collected a lot of notes, theories, techniques and stories on the paranormal subject and it was a number of years ago I began to piece it all together in the hope that my notes could help budding ghost hunters or professionals looking for new theories on investigating.

So this book is for you. I hope you learn, laugh and get a bit spooked. I hope that you get a great insight into the paranormal and enjoy hearing some of my own experiences.

Now in 2014 I can look back at the last eleven years and look at how far I have come along with my research and investigation in that time. I have grown up with the paranormal and made some of my closest friends because of it. I am very much aware now that I have spent so long living with the paranormal it is slowly becoming normal to me!

On a final note, while leaving a ghost hunt at Tutbury Castle with Lesley one morning at 3am she turned to me and said "I'm sure there are easier ways to make a living!" I'm sure there are Lesley, but where's the fun and screaming in that!

PART I
EXPLAINGING THE UNEXPLAINED

JAMES WARRENDER

GHOSTS & SPIRITS

Before we begin to look at the history of Ghosts & Spirits, first I would like to define them.

Ghost: *"An apparition of a dead person that is believed to appear or become visable to the living, typically as a nebulous image."*

Spirit: *"The non physical part of a person that is the seat of emotions and character; the soul."*

Some believe a ghost may be seen and can communicate with the living and it is often said to be like a recording, while a spirit can have feelings attached to it and is more active than a ghost.

In my experience a spirit is what I would call "active" and it is spirit entities that can move a table during a table tipping session or communicate through a Ouija Board. A ghost is simply like watching a DVD. It is a recording of something that was once live and can be replayed over and over again, reliving what it once lived. Now we will have a look at a very brief history of Ghosts and Sprits.

If you look back through history, ghosts are everywhere. While the Victorian era Spiritualism Movement popularised ghosts in the modern era and in Western culture you can actually track ghost sightings to prehistory. Stone Age cave paintings found in Indonesia and South America depict ghostly figures and spectres which date back between 10,000 and 15,000 years respectively.

Ghosts also feature in early Mesopotamian religions, specifically in the religions of

Babylon and Assyria and other early states in Mesopotamia. Investigating further you can find traces of these beliefs in later Abrahamic religions. These religions would speak of visitations from sectors known as "Gidim" and "Etemmu" Their belief was that Ghosts were created at the moment of death and would hold on to the personality and memory of the person, like a photograph. Families were expected to make offerings to the dead and worship them to make their time in the afterlife easier.

The common belief in Babylon at the time was that ghosts could contact any living person and if you suffered from headaches, earaches, sight problems, dizziness and just about any other health related issue this was a sure sign that a ghost was making contact.

While in Classical Antiquity ghosts were known as "Shade" and in fact a "Shade" makes an appearance in the First Book of Samuel in the Old Testament. Moreover during the periods of Archaic and Classical

Greek, ghosts appear more including in Homer's Odyssey and Iliad in which they are described as: *"...a vapour, gibbering and whining into earth"*

Moving forward and looking at the Roman Empire, people believed that ghosts could be used to take revenge on their enemies. All you had to do was carve a curse onto a piece of wood, stone or lead and place into an open grave. A ghost would then haunt and torment the person quite literally to death.

A reported and popular ghost story of the time was recorded at the Baths at Chaeronea in the 1st Century. The ghost of a murdered man would walk the area filling the air with loud frightful groans which caused the people that lived there too seal up the doors to their homes, fearful that the ghost would come inside. Another ghost story, documented to have happened around 50 years later by Pliny The Younger who wrote of a ghostly man in chains who would terrorize people with screams and other nasty shocks. Some men braved the spirit one evening and followed him where he pointed to the ground. The men began to dig and they found the body of a man in shackles who had been murdered. They reburied him properly and the haunting soon stopped.

When we arrive in the 5th Century, ghosts had become feared creatures, haunting and evil. Less religious than in the past and more focused on something to be afraid of. It is in the 5th Century that ghosts first appear in fiction. The play, by Aeschylus features the "Ghost of Clytemnestra" who in true ghostly style appears "exactly how or from where is uncertain" and leaves "As the first of them begins to awake".

The middle ages once again brought a change as to how ghosts were represented in literature. In fact, ghosts became more psychical beings and they could be classified into two categories. Either 'Souls of the Dead' or 'Demons'. Demons were sent to tempt and scare the living while Souls of the Dead were sent to protect and warn the living. Or sometimes they were stuck on earth. So psychical were some ghosts many reports suggest that they were tied or chained up while a Priest was sent for to hear the ghost's confession before they could be released to the other side. An interesting point to note: most, if not all of reported Middle Aged ghost sightings were of male spirits.

The Middle Ages also brought a number of reports of Ghostly Armies. Something that is still a common sighting today. Two well known cases both come from 1211 from around the Wandlebury area of England. The first tells of three living Knights were challenged to duels by a Knights that had died in battles many weeks or in some cases years previously. The second story came from a Gervase of Tilbury who witnessed a ghostly boy being attacked by a group of Knights.

Once again we can move forward, this time to ghosts in the Renaissance era where we begin to see a rise in the popularity of the occult and necromancy but also a large backlash to the subject, which included many Witch Trials for people that claimed to see ghosts. Despite the trials the era also saw the depiction of supernatural creatures in Art and more so in Literature. A popular children's rhyme from the time "Sweet William's Ghost" tells the story of a man returning to haunt his fiancé who he could now no longer marry to ask her to release him from their engagement otherwise he will face eternal damnation.

*"There came a ghost to Margaret's door,
With many a grievous grone,
And ay he tirled at the pin;
But answer made she none..."*

Author Raymond Nighan discusses in greater depth in his book "Renaissance Ghosts and Demons" what people of that time thought a ghost could be:

"An hallucination (phantasma) brought about by stress, poor diet, or exhaustion. A specter seen as a portent or omen, a spirit of a dead person returned to perform some deed left undone in life, a spirit of a dead person returned from the grave or from

purgatory by divine permission (the Catholic position), an angel disguised as a dead person, or a devil disguised as a dead person to tempt a living relative into eternal damnation"

Moving forward once again we arrive at the what many could arguably say was the most popular time for ghosts and spirits. The Victorian Spiritualism Movement. The movement was most prominent between 1820 and 1920 and again in during the Second World War. The movement was triggered by the Fox Sisters who claimed that they could make spirits manifest themselves in the form of tapping around a table. They became popular worldwide and would tour with their "Spirit Rapping" show.

The success of the sisters brought forward a number of other mediums who would hold Séances and invite people to come and see the show to demonstrate their abilities. The 1900s also saw an increase in the number of ghost stories that began to circulate and helped make the subject of ghosts even more popular.

As the 1930s and 1940s drew to a close the "Modern Ghost Hunter" born. People like Harry Price and Hanz Holzer popularised the ideas of Ghost Hunting. While the 1940's saw an increase in people visiting mediums to get help in reaching out to family members they had lost during the War. The 1950s which brought television meant that a new medium (no pun intended) could be utilised to exhibit ghosts. American TV stations broadcast live ghost hunts during the 1950s right through to the 1970s, including Hanz Holzer's investigation in the Amityville House.

Cinema also depicted ghosts and the paranormal. Films such as *'The Exorcist'* frightened viewers into believing in a life after death (and in some cases into believing in a God and a Devil). Move forward ten years and ghosts became immortalized forever with the popular film *"Ghostbusters"* which introduced ghosts to an entirely new, world wide audience and made ghosts almost a fun acceptable subject.

The 1990s and Early 2000s reintroduced ghosts into television with the rising numbers of mediums appearing on TV shows and a rise in programmes which investigated the topic. Now there are full TV channels dedicated to ghosts and 24 hour psychic hotlines run on air.

Looking back through history we will see that ghosts began as religious symbols and soon became a form of entertainment. They became things to fear and to watch out for before being used for entertainment once again and has time has moved on people have become more understanding of ghosts and are more willing to accept them into our lifestyle.

POLTERGEISTS

"A ghost or other supernatural being supposedly responsible for physical disturbances such as making loud noises and throwing objects about."

Poltergeist comes from the German words Poltern "to make sound" and Geist "ghost or spirit" They are often said to be a malicious or evil spirit which can haunt either a specific location or person. They have been reported all over the world many times dating back over 1000 years. Poltergeists are known to throw objects, make loud knocking sounds, start small fires, make water appear from no where and physically touch, hit or scratch people.

While some have even been known to speak or make contact with the living.

The first reported case was in circa 858 AD where a family in a Germanic farm house reported their home was being bombarded with stones and terribly loud knocking and banging on the walls which lasted all through the day and night. It would also knock over beds causing the family to be thrown to the ground in pain.

In the 1970s an American parapsychologist undertook a study of over 400 reported Poltergeist cases. He found that:

- 64% were capable of moving small objects.

- 58% were most active at night.

- 48% could make banging noises on walls.

- 36% could over larger objects.

- 24% reported the activity lasted for over a year.

- 16% could be communicated with.

- 12% could open and shut doors.

Moreover, a study of half of the investigated cases showed:

- 15% scratched people.

- 11% started small fires.

- 5% could produce unexplained pools of water.

For hundreds of years it was thought that Poltergeists were demons caused by witches or from a witches curse due to the religious influence at the time. Another theory was that Poltergeists were caused by someone killed in an angry or violent death. Their death caused a "mark" which would affect the surrounding area and replay or release the feelings at the time of death.

In more modern times different investigations into Poltergeists has discovered that Psycho kinesis Energy could be the cause of such activity. By which they mean that someone's emotional, stress or anxiety levels could be played out through items being influenced.

A study of 116 poltergeist cases carried about by psychologist and parapsychologist William G. Roll showed that the "vast majority" of poltergeist cases were centred around or heavily featured children or teenagers – making this age range a high point for high emotions and energy in what Roll described as Recurrent Spontaneous Psycho kinesis.

There are said to be 7 key stages of Poltergeist Activity:

1 – Disappearing Objects

In recent times people report that their keys or mobile phones go missing. Only for them to turn up days, weeks or months later in the exact place they would normally be found. Or sometimes the items may be found somewhere entirely different such as in a shoe box in the wardrobe or high on a bookshelf.

2 – Objects Levitating or Thrown

This can range from anything including mugs or plates sliding across tables, chairs tipping over when no one is sitting on them and drawers opening and closing. It can range from the littlest items to pieces or furniture moving across a room.

3 – Scents and Odours

These can include a strong smell of tobacco in the house which would be odd if no one in the house smokes or maybe the strong smell of flowers which can arise from no where. Although common with poltergeists, this activity can also be connected to a few other types of haunting.

4 – Electrical Interference

This can come in the form of batteries draining very quickly, sometimes ones that are newly out of the packet, or items which are fully charged draining from 100 to 0 in a matter of moments.

5 – Power From No Where

Examples of this include old watches which haven't worked for decades suddenly springing to life or children's toys suddenly turning themselves on during the night, in some reported cases of this happening parents have picked up the toys to switch them off only to discover there aren't any batteries in the toy.

6 – Knocks, Footsteps and Other Noises

These are sounds that aren't linked to the natural sounds the house or building would normally make. There could be a pattern to these sounds or it could just be a one or two time only event. Phantom conversations have also been reported in poltergeist cases. People have sometimes heard full conversations which suddenly stop when they go to investigate.

7 – Psychical Attacks

This can range from anything from being tugged or pinched by a poltergeist, there have been more extreme cases where people have been slapped, punched, scratched, cut and sometimes even thrown across a room.

For further reading, there are famous Poltergeist cases including: Borley Rectory, the Rosenheim Poltergeist, The Black Monk of Pontefract, The Enfield Poltergeist

(1977), Drummer of Tedworth (1662), The Bell Witch of Tennessee (1817–1872), The Fox Sisters (1848), Great Amherst Mystery (1878–79), Epworth Rectory, Gef the Talking Mongoose (1931), Robbie Mannheim (1949), The Thornton Road poltergeist of Birmingham (1981), Tina Resch (1984), "The Stone-Throwing Spook of Little Dixie" (1995), The Canneto di Caronia fires poltergeist (2004–5) and The Miami Poltergeist (2008).

Poltergeists cases have increased over the last 30 years or so. Could this be because of a high level of paranormal activity across the world? Or are films such as "Poltergeist" (1980) and the more recent "Paranormal Activity" (2009 –) series fuelling people's imaginations.

JAMES WARRENDER

ELECTRONIC VOICE PHENOMENA

"Sounds found on electronic recordings which resemble speech, but are not the result of intentional recording or rendering. EVP are commonly found in recordings with static, stray radio transmissions, and background noise."

Electronic Voice Phenomena or EVP has been a popular method of spirit communication for around the last 70 years. With the advancement of sound recording equipment EVP based investigations have become more common in the last ten years.

Among the first people to attempt EVP recording was Attila Von Szalay, a Swedish Photographer. He specialised in spirit photography and began to investigate the idea of using sound recordings to hear the voices of the spirits he had photographed and hoped that the voices could guide him to where he should photograph next. He began by using a 78 RPM recorder in as early as 1941 but he reported he didn't have much success until he switched to a reel-to-reel tape recorder in 1956.

Von Szalay worked closely with Raymond Bayless, who was psychologist and paranormal investigator. Together they built a devise consisting of a microphone in an insulated cabinet connected to an external recording device and speaker. They reported that at times you could get full spirit communication through the device which they didn't hear in the room at the time. They called the spirit voices "discarnate speakers".

Among some of the first recorded voices that Von Szalay and Bayless captured were of a woman's voice saying: "This is G", "Hot

Dog, Art" and "Merry Christmas and a Happy New Year to You All"

A famous case in 1959 was of a artist who would record bird sounds in the woods beside where he stayed. Upon listening back to the recordings, he discovered the voice of his dead Father had been picked up. Further recordings also resulted in him capturing the voices of his Mother and Wife.

Another prominent EVP recorder was Konstantin Raudive. He was a Latvian psychologist who taught at the University of Uppsala in Sweden. He, with the help of a home made recording device, captured over 10,000 voices that belonged to the dead. Some were captured under Screened Laboratory conditions and the words that were spoken were easily identifiable to Raudive. He invited thousands of people to come and to the recordings and many believed that the voices could not be explained by ordinary means.

Many people attempted to make their own recorders after the success of others in the field, but it wasn't until the late 1980s that another breakthrough was made. William O'Neil made the "Spiricom" with instructions left for him by George Mueller – a scientist, over six years before. The device was said to offer a two way conversation between the living and the dead.

While O'Neil was successful, he offered the design out for free to anyone who wished to try it for themselves. No one claimed as good a success as O'Neil got.

The idea of the "Spiricom" is said to have inspired Frank Sumption, an American paranormal investigator to make the "Franks Box" which is a device that claims to offer a real-time conversation between the living and the dead. White noise is used on an AM band radio which has been modified to sweep between the empty frequencies giving snippets of sound that are meant to be ghostly voices.

In more recent years a paranormal investigator created the Ovilus, a device which reacts to environmental factors, including EMF, and turns the readings into words. The idea behind being that spirits can manipulate the environment allowing them to speak through the box.

There have been mixed reviews with these sort of devises, but the overall consensus is that it does work and with upgrades being released more often that the paranormal industry is getting closer than ever to making contact through sound.

JAMES WARRENDER

MEDIUMSHIP

"Mediumship, or channelling, is the practice of certain people—known as mediums—to purportedly mediate communication between spirits of the dead and other human beings."

Mediumship is currently a very popular method of paranormal investigation – with every paranormal team around the country having one, two or even three mediums involved with each investigation. While an interest in Mediumship has been around since early human history, it is in the last 200 years, with the 19th Century Spiritualism movement, platform Mediumship and Television that interest has boomed.

There are five different types of Mediumship:

- Channelling

This is the most common, where the medium, sometimes with the help of a spirit guide will relay messages to the living.

- Mental Mediumship

Someone that can link, tap or tune in to the spirit world by listening, sensing or seeing spirits.

- Trance Mediumship

Where a medium will allow the spirit to communicate using their mind and will often include some form of automatic writing or manipulation of a voice box to hear a spirit talk.

- Physical Mediumship

This is where a spirit, through a medium can appear through ectoplasm, cause knocking or rapping sounds, ring bells or affect other people in a room.

- Demonstrative

Normally this will take place in front of audiences and will incorporate another form of Mediumship as well.

Within Mediumship, different mediums can sense different things in different ways. There are seven ways in which the mediums will know of a spirit's presence.

- Clairvoyance: the art of Clear Seeing, where a medium will see a full apparition of a spirit within the mind's eye.

- Clairaudience: the art of Clear Hearing, where a medium will hear spirits. It may be the spirit's voice directly or through a spirit guide.

- Clairsentience: the art of Clear Sensing, where a medium will get the impression a spirit wishes to communicate or will feel sensations passed onto them by spirit.

- Clairsentience, the art of Clear Feeling, where the medium will take on the condition of a sprit, possibly a disability or illness.

- Clairalience, the art of Clear Smelling, where a medium will smell a spirit, possibly their pipe tobacco or a perfume.

- Clairgustance, the art of Clear Tasting, where a medium will get taste impressions from spirit.

- Claircognizance, the art of Clear Knowing, where a medium will get a sense of something that doesn't come through a normal psychic means.

One of the earliest cases of Mediumship comes from the story of the Witch of Endor who raised the spirit of the dead Prophet Samuel to allow the Hebrew King Saul to question his former mentor about an upcoming battle. This appears in the First Book of Samuel in the Old Testament.

Very little can be found on Mediumship again until the 12th Century during the Renaissance when a law was past prohibiting "mystics and psychics" from performing on the streets.

It was in the late 19th Century that Mediumship became popular once again with the Fox Sisters. They were joined by other prominent Trance Mediums including Paschal Beverly Randolph (1825 – 1875), a medical doctor turned medium and Emma Hardinge Britten (1823 – 1899) in advancing the Spiritualism Movement by touring the world performing their Mediumship abilities. It was a teacher, Allan Kardec, who coined the terms Spiritualism and Mediumship in his five books written on the subjects.

Mediumship saw a surge of interest in the 1940s during World War II with families and grieving widows who would reach out to mediums to help contact their family members that had been killed in the war. Most famously during this time was the medium Helen Duncan who was the last person to be arrested under the Witchcraft Act of 1735 due to her readings.

During a trance, Helen had spoken of the sinking of the HMS Barham, this information had only been released via the Government to the families of those involved – only at the start of the following year did the news break to the world.

Duncan's knowledge of this information caused her to be arrested and held in jail for 9 months. Upon her release the Witchcraft Act of 1735 was abolished.

Mediumship began a slow decline in the 1950s and it wouldn't be for another 40 years that the interest would be reignited with the help of television. Mediums such as Derek Acorah, Mia Dolan and Tony Stockwell all helped bring back Mediumship to the masses in the modern day.

EXTRASENSORY PERCEPTION

"The supposed faculty of perceiving things by means other than the known senses, e.g. by telepathy."

Extrasensory Perception or ESP has been studied in great detail over the last 150 years. It was one of the first paranormal areas to be properly studied in science. It aims to investigate claims of receiving information through the mind, passed telepathically. In particular, many mediums claim to have this ability.

Studies of ESP can be traced as far back as 1870 when the phrase was coined by an explorer, Sir Richard Burton. The studies were later brought to the United Kingdom where the Society of Psychical Research spent a great deal of time surveying people about the reported ability. Their reports at the time were found to be inconclusive.

Reports show that in France in 1892, Dr Paul Joire, a medical doctor and researcher conducted a number of experiments and felt that ESP was a state, brought on by hypnotism or in a deep trance could receive information that was being sent telepathically without the use of the ordinary scenes.

Breakthrough studies were conducted in the 1930s by JB Rhine and his wife Louisa. They tried to develop ESP into an experimental science. To avoid the usual connotations of hauntings and séances they decided to name it parapsychology. While JB worked on defining terms such as ESP and psi (energy transfer), Louisa spent time working on cases and examined results.

The couple then invented the Zener Cards, a series of five cards with a circle, square, wavy lines, cross and a star on them. There would be five cards to each shape which would be randomly shuffled and the host of the experiment, the "sender", would concentrate on the shape and attempt to send it to the "receiver". They decided that anything above 60% would be a definite sign of ESP. They also held a Clairvoyance test where the deck of cards would be "closed" and the "receiver" would have to use their abilities to guess the correct shape on the card.

Rhine's later research included an independent survey of all official and recorded ESP tests throughout history. He concluded that 61% or more reported significant results, suggestive of ESP.

Future investigations held by Rhine included looking at whether dogs could sense landmines using their own ESP. He had a number of dogs trained for over three months and the final results revealed that six out of seven times the dogs were successful at finding landmines without the use of any other senses.

By the end of his life, JB Rhine had over 75

publications of his and Louisa's ESP research and investigations. He his still held as one of the most prominent figures in parapsychology research.

In 1964 another independent research mission was held where people would be hypnotised and asked to reveal what images were coming to them. In this case there was more than a 64% success rate.

1974 saw Edgar Dean Mitchell of the Apollo 14 moon landing mission attempt his own ESP Investigations from Space. Mitchell took his own set of Zener Cards into space where with the help of a radio link was able to test the ground control team. Mitchell's results are inconclusive. Today Mitchell is well known for discussing UFOs and other paranormal occurrences.

Based on the experiments of Wolfgang Metzger, a technique known as the Ganzfeld Theory was used in ESP investigations from around 1971. The technique involved cutting off the senses by: having the subject's eyes covered by half ping-pong balls and having a red light shone at them and their ears covered by headphones which would play in white noise. The subject would then be asked to use free association (automatic writing) to draw or write what had come to them. In another room there would be a "sender" concentrating on the image, hopefully passing it to the subject who would then draw it or write what they are seeing. During the first attempts at this experiment, there was a 37% hit rate.

A further 1984 test by Gertrude Schmeidler, confirmed to investigators that subjects who had been hypnotised had a much higher success rate that those who had not. The same investigator carried out further tests in 1988 and discovered that those who were tested by a "friendly" investigator had better success rates that those who were tested by an "angry" investigator.

She also determined that in an experiment, those who were branded "sheep" and had been told that ESP would work scored a much, much higher success rate than those labelled "goats" and had been told that it wouldn't work. Sometimes a more than

50% margin was noticed.

Most recently, a test carried out in 2011 by Professor Daryl Bem of Cornwall University is said to have concluded that out of nine experiments that he had carried out over the past ten years showed that humans could accurately predict random events.

There are still ongoing investigations into ESP and a number of online experiments urge the public to get involved to help gain a broader picture of ESP. This author scored 16.67% , 8% below the national average and 44% below the margin for a definite sign of ESP!

SÉANCE

"A meeting at which people attempt to make contact with the dead, especially through the agency of a medium."

Séance comes from a French word "séance" which translates to "sitting", "session" or "seat".

No one can be quite sure where the séance originated but it can be traced back as early as 1760 in the book "Communication with the Other Side" written by George First Baron Lyttelton, a notable Politian who was the Chancellor of the Exchequer to Prime Minister Thomas Pelham-Holles (1754 – 1756, 1757 – 1762). In his works, he claimed to have made contact with Peter the Great, Pericles, William Penn and Christina, Queen of Sweden.

The popularity of the séance grew in the late 19th Century with the growth of Spiritualism. News of séances held by The Fox Sisters, The Davenport Brothers and mediums such as Achsa W Sprague, Emma Hardinge Britten and Cora Scott Hatch captured the world's interest and made the séance the trend of the time. It later became a popular after dinner parlour game.

For a long time and even still to this day many have argued that the 16th President of the USA. Abraham Lincoln was an occultist. This was because of his keen interest in Spiritualism and séances.

In March 1861, Lincoln and his wife Mary Todd took over the White House and almost instantly they began to experience the ghosts of former presidents there. The first séance they held in the White House took place a few weeks after their young son died. In a state of grief, Mary Todd consulted mediums and began séances with her husband.

It is said that during a séance in 1861, Lincoln made contact with Henry Knox, George Washington's Secretary of War and asked advice on how to end the American Civil War. This séance was held in the presence of a reporter from the Boston Gazette and made headline news.

Interestingly, it was during a séance that Lincoln was told that he should sign the Emancipation Proclamation, the freedom of slaves in the states still in rebellion; as if he did he would go down in history for it. Lincoln had his doubts about signing the declaration before this but the message caused him to change is mind. It comes as no surprise that even now the ghost of Lincoln is still sighted in the White House from time to time.

There are four different types of séance that can be held:

- Religious Séance

This would be held in a Spiritualism church and while it is not seen as a traditional form of a séance it would involve a gifted medium receiving and relaying messages to the dead in front of a congregation. It would also involve an almost traditional Christian service including the singing of hymns. It would often be known as a Demonstration of the Continuation of Life. This type of séance could also be held to make contact with people linked to the church in the hope they could tell the sitters what the afterlife is like.

- Stage Mediumship Séance

Much like a religions séance, a medium would take to the stage in front of a crowd but this wouldn't involve any religious aspects to it. These types of séances are more common today featuring mediums that tour the country demonstrating their abilities.

- Leader Assisted Séance

These are the most commonly depicted séances. It would involve a small group of people, possibly in the dark, holding hands in a circle. They would be lead by a medium that would go into a trance or possibly use automatic writing to make contact with the dead. Once commutation has been established it is common for the spirit to then be asked to interact with people or objects within the room. During Victorian séances, a red light would be used as it is a popular theory that spirits can be seen easier in red lights.

- Informal Social Séance

This type of séance would most likely be seen at after dinner parties. Many would do them for fun and it is often said they are done with two or three people and no medium or other leader. Sometimes they are done by young people to test the barrier between the living and the dead.

As Spiritualism grew many people began to experiment with the séance and tried to introduce a number of different items and objects for spirits to interact with. The first was a spirit horn which was a long metal tube to be left on the séance table. It is said that it would magnify the whispered voices of the dead.

Spirit Slates were also introduced. These were two chalkboards which were tied together and left alone while the séance took place. Afterwards they would be untied and would often have messages written on them, supposedly left by spirits.

Séance Tables would also come into use. These were especially made very light weight tables that would be easier for spirits to move. These tables would turn, levitate and shake in the presence of a medium.

Finally, the Spirit Cabinet was introduced. This was a portable cabinet which a medium would sit inside and then be tied into. This was to stop them from manipulating other objects but also said to help them reach a deeper state of trance by cutting them off from others.

Modern paranormal investigators continue to use the séance to this day.

OUIJA BOARD

"A board with letters, numbers, and other signs around its edge, to which a planchette, movable pointer, or upturned glass moves, supposedly in answer to questions from people at a séance."

The use of the Ouija Board can be traced back to China, as far back as 1100AD to the Song Dynasty. It was known as "Fuji" and was described as a type of "planchette writing" done only under specific conditions or special rituals. It was often taught in some schools until it became forbidden during the Qing Dynasty some time later.

Other cultures used the board during this time including: Ancient Grease, India, Rome and Medieval Europe. The boards were often seen as something demonic and unholy. Many religions and cultures banned their use, claiming it was the work of Satan.

It wasn't until the late 19th Century when the Spiritualist Movement occurred that the now commonly seen Ouija Board was introduced. With the likes of the Fox Sisters and other prominent mediums of the day speaking of the new "talking boards" it was only a matter of time before it too, like the séance, became a well known after-dinner game.

Elijah Bond and Charlie Kennard produced the Ouija Board as it is known today but not as a tool to aid paranormal investigation, but as a toy. They first went on sale on 28 May, 1890 and was simply called Ouija. It was said to be called Ouija because it was the Ancient Egyptian word meaning "luck". It was some time after it was argued that it comes from the French and German words for "yes".

In the early 1900s William Fuld took over the production of the boards but began to market them as more of a paranormal tool than a toy. He is often named the Father of the Modern Day Ouija". This title was short lived for Fuld as in 1927 he fell three storeys from his office building while trying to fix a flag pole that was outside his window. Some argue that Fuld committed suicide after receiving messaged through a board. Others say he was possessed by a demonic spirit that spoke with him through the board.

After Fuld's death the production of the Ouija Board fell into the hands of the Parker Brothers, who also produced Monopoly and Cluedo (Clue in the USA). They returned production back to being that of a toy. Currently today there are as many as ten different types of Ouija Board still in production and readily available across the world.

The Ouija Board is still seen as dangerous with a number of people reporting that it can cause anything from depression to the death of the people using it.

Recently the boards were burned in Alamogordo in New Mexico by fundamentalist groups as they were a sign of witchcraft and devil worship that held information that should only be available to God.

Bishops in Micronesia pushed for them to be banned as they felt they were bad and that they were the portals to speak to demons. Many would hold lectures on the evils of the board and insisted that people should stay away from them.

The debate on the safety of the board varies from person to person. Some believe that they are the single most dangerous item a paranormal investigator or a person can use, while others feel they are vital to paranormal investigation.

Personally I feel they aren't dangerous when done correctly with the necessary protection rituals done before and after it. I also feel it comes down to each person's perception of the boards. If you feel they are negative devices, you will find a way to leave with a negative perception of them. If you feel they are good and interesting, you will leave with positive reflections on them.

That said there are a number of stories of people being so affected by using the boards they may act on the feelings and will sometimes become depressed, ill or in some extreme cases, take their own lives.

Throughout history there have been a number of famous people who have claimed that the board has had a large influence in their career.

- The singer Alice Cooper is said to have got his stage name while conducting a Ouija board session. During it he was told he is the reincarnation of a witch named Alice Cooper. The story interested him so much he decided to use the name for his rock persona.

- In 1917 an author named Emily Grant Hutching wrote an entire book that she claimed was dictated to her by Mark Twain via the Ouija Board.

- The author Sylvia Plath wrote "Dialogue Over A Ouija Board" which was entirely based on her experiences on using the board.

Today the Ouija Board is used by paranormal investigators across the country and in the last decade it has become almost as popular again as it was 200 years ago. Believers and Skeptics alike can all agree that the Ouija certainly does have something strange within it, but what that is, we can never be sure.

TABLE TIPPING

"The manipulation of a table during a séance; attributed to spirits"

Table Tipping or Table Turning is a type of séance where people will sit around a table with their hands lightly touching upon the table top, someone will call out the letters of the alphabet and the table is said to move in correspondence to the letter. A more traditional method will see the sitters simply place their hands on the table and ask for the spirits to manipulate or move the table.

Much like the séance and the Ouija Board, Table Tipping became popular when the Spiritualist Movement hit Europe in 1852.

Many early attempts at Table Tipping saw the table shake, float or slide around the room. It originated in the USA in 1848 but when medium, Maria B Hayden first demonstrated it in England and later France, it really became a common interest. So much so the French phrase "Comment est votre tableau turining" (translating to: How's your table turning) meaning "how are you?" became popular and well used.

As with many other paranormal investigation experiments it was deemed demonic and that it was "under Satan's influence", but many scientists began to investigate Table Tipping as well. They believed the movement of the table, outside of any obvious fraud, was coming from an energy produced by the participants themselves. Both Count Agenor De Gasparin and Professor Marc Thury of Geneva held a number of Table Tipping Sessions and came to the conclusion that the force was in fact caused by the participants – it became known as Ectenic Force. Other scientists argued it was either:

group hypnosis, power of suggestion, someone moving it, electricity or even movement of the earth that caused the table to move.

The public ignored what the scientists reported and continued to practice Table Tipping, some for genuine paranormal interest – others for after dinner games or light entertainment.

A commonly believed theory on Table Tipping, based on a number of historical paranormal investigators and current ones is, the more the same group of people conduct Table Tipping, the quicker the activity will build and the more violent the table will move. This can be reported at random times out with investigations as well. A reporter, Gambier Bolton in early 1904 was having dinner with medium, Florence Cook. He reported that the table, a large, heavy oak one, slid across the floor and began to spin out of control on its own. The paranormal investigator Harry Price once reported a table shaking so violently while in a restaurant with is wife that it broke in two.

In the late Victorian Era, Table Tipping began to die down in popularity with the popularity of the Ouija Board and Planchette.

Today Table Tipping is used by paranormal investigators across the world to attempt communication with the dead, due to its simplicity and sometimes exciting results and with the surge of television programmes about paranormal investigation who attempt Table Tipping, it is growing more popular each year.

GLASS DIVINATION

"The use of a glass upside down with two or more people's fingers lightly pressed upon it, then asking for spirit to make communication"

Glass Divination, Glass Moving or Glass Divining is when participants will place their fingers on an upturned glass and use traditional calling out methods to attempt to get spirits to move the glass.

The use of Glass Divination and Divination itself can be traced back through history and features in various cultures and religions, most prominently in Ancient

Greece. Oracles and Seers practiced divination with their own Gods to gain insight into the future and sometimes held divining sessions before a battle to receive advice on how to win it or to even see the outcome.

In later Religions it was seen as bad. The Hebrew Bible forbids any type of divination as it is seen as one detesting and mistrusting the words of God. In Christianity it was considered a Pagan Practice and if you were found to be practicing it you could be tried and even sentenced to death for going against God. The Catholic Church passed cannon laws to prohibit people from practising divination.

The use of Divination became popular in the middle ages with many charging to have their future told via divining. This soon stopped happening when various witchcraft laws and trials came into practice and Capital Punishment could be enforced if you were found to be divining.

Glass Divination became one of the earliest forms of spiritual communication with some sources pre-dating the spiritualist movement. Many felt it was a very successful form of communication as it offered answers to questions that couldn't be answered before this time. Mediums and Psychics have warned in the past about using the glass after a divining session as it may be tainted by evil spirits and make someone unwell.

The widely reported issue with Glass Divination is that of static friction where the glass may stick to the table and be unable to move. The way this is overcome is for the group to move the glass and then ask for spirits to manipulate the movement into a shape or movement relevant to the answer.

With the growth of the Spiritualism movement, the popularity of Glass Divination also grew as another method of paranormal investigation which is still practiced today.

JAMES WARRENDER

ORBS

"A spherical object, shape or ball of light caught on photograph or video, said to be the first stage of a ghostly apparition."

Orbs are widely reported around the world in photographs and in film. Many would say they are the first stage of a spirit manifestation. There is great debate, especially with the advancement in examination technology, just what orbs are. Many would argue they are spirit, while others say they are just bits of dust or small insects getting caught in the camera flash.

Paranormal Investigators would argue they are spirits but more specifically the souls of those who don't wish to cross into the spirit world and have stayed through fear of being judged.

The reports of Orbs became more popular with the invention of digital photography, with cameras with built in flash and when people could instantly look back at the photo they had just taken. This was used by paranormal investigators who began to notice the small balls of light.

Stages of an Orb Manifestation

1 – Orb. A small ball of light, often seen in different colours and sizes.

2 – Vortex. Long, snake like shape of misty light. Sometimes seen in various shapes and moving in different directions

3 – Ectoplasm. As energy grows spirit may take on foggy mist or form of a person or different shapes.

4 – Apparition. A full body appearance of a spirit.

A location is said to be more haunted if people can see orbs with the naked eye. Once again these visible orbs are put down to corner of the eye phenomena or again just specs of dust.

At one stage orbs were seen as the step forward in paranormal investigation. But now the are mostly ignored by people in the industry as a rational explanation has been discovered.

JAMES WARRENDER

DOWSING RODS

"Divining rod: forked stick that is said to dip down to indicate underground water or oil or used to detect a paranormal presence"

Originally Dowsing Rods were used to find water, buried metals or gem stones or to find gravesites. In the last fifty years they have been used by paranormal researchers to aid their investigations.

The rods were seen as "Y" shaped sticks which are freshly cut from trees. The two pointed ends are held with the long bit out in front. The dowser then has to walk and when the long branch dips or makes an obvious movement a discovery has been found. This is also known as "Willow Witching".

Today the rods are more commonly seen as "L" shaped and the dowser will have two rods. When a discovery is made the rods will cross over or move a part.

Dowsing can be traced back to Germany during the 15th Century. They were used to find metals. Martin Luther later listed dowsing as wrong as it was seen as going against religion and God. In 1662 it was seen as Satanic and superstitious. Some even suggested that the Devil was responsible for moving the rods.

They were next commonly used in the early 19th Century in South Dakota where people would use them to find water or wells in their land. They become popular again during the Vietnam War where they would be used to locate weapons, mines and tunnels. They were most recently used by an Army in 1986 when an avalanche covered 31 Norwegian Soldiers. The rods were used in their rescue mission.

The "L" shaped rods are the ones most commonly used by paranormal investigators today. To begin with the dowser will establish how the rods will move if a spirit is present. Sometimes crossing will mean yes, going a part will mean no or vice versa. It will differ from person to person.

Out of many years of research many investigators will say that brass or copper are the best type of rods to use as they will become in tune to magnetic fields.

It is not just rods that are used for dowsing. Many have used and still do use a pendulum which is an object attached to a rope or chain that will swing freely and is open to spirit manipulation.

The pendulum can be a metal or crystal weight and different crystals will have a different affect depending on the type of crystal or the strength of the spirit that is doing the manipulation.

The investigator or dowser will ask a yes/no question and after establishing the movement related to the answer, they will be able to have a question and answer session. In some cases they may call out the letters of the alphabet and watch for which letter the pendulum will move on.

Dowsing is seen as a very interesting tool and one that many ghost hunters around the world still use today.

TAROT CARDS

"A deck of cards that include 22 images representing virtues, vices, death and fortune etc.; used by fortune-tellers"

Tarot Cards are commonly used tools by psychics, mediums and paranormal investigators from around the world. The word Tarot comes from the Italian word Tarocchi which has no known origin. Some have speculated it may have links to the Taro River in Parma. It may even have links to the Arabic word Turuq meaning "ways". The cards are used to gain insight into the past, present or future by being guided by spirits through the cards.

Originally the cards were made to be a simple game, much like playing cards today. No one can be really sure where the game originated from, but many feel they have links to Ancient Egypt. The cards remained a game until a French occultist began to tell fortunes with them in the 1770s.

The earliest reference to the cards in an occult form is from the 16th – 17th Centuries where Dominican Preachers would give sermons on the "Devil's Picture Book" and the evils of the cards which were being used for divining methods.

In 1781 Antoine Court De Gébelin, a Swiss Clergyman and Freemason began researching the Cards and in his book "Le Monde Primitif" he speculated the theories that the cards held religious, occult and other mysterious symbols and meanings. He also claimed that Tarot came from the Ancient Egyptian word "Tor" meaning Royal or Road so the cards represented the Road to Royalty.

De Gébelin found in his research that the cards were:

- Of mystical Cabbalistic importance

- Of deep divine significance

- A book of eternal medicine

- An account of the creation of the world

- That the first sets of Tarot Cards were printed on leaves of gold.

With his research complete, De Gébelin began work on his own set of Tarot Cards with his own interpretation of what they should represent.

Battler – Will

High Priestess – Knowledge

Empress – Action

Emperor – Realisation

Chief Hierophant – Occult Inspiration

Marriage – Ordeal

Osiris Triumphant – Victory

Justice – Equilibrium

Wise Man – Wisdom

Wheel of Fortune – Future

Fortitude – Strength

Prudence – Sacrifice

Death – Transformation

Devil – Fate

The Castle – Ruin

Star – Hope

Moon – Deception

Sun – Happiness

Creation – Renewal

Time – Reward

These interpretations are almost exactly what are still used to this day in Tarot Cards and were the most commonly used deck through the recent centuries. They were regularly used by gypsies who would charge people to hear their fortunes being read. The cards were and often still are marvelled for their accuracy as well as their magical, mystical and psychological effect.

Today, while being used by mediums and psychics the reader will shuffle the deck, place the cards out in "spreads" and interpret them for the reader. There are number of "spreads" still used today including the Five Card Spread, The Ellipse, The Celtic, The Mirror, The Mandala and the Relationship. Each "spread" will represent a different type of reading for the cards.

A number of paranormal groups will use the cards to attempt to read a reportedly haunted building. The same "spreads" may be used and the reader will interpret the cards in regards to the building they are in.

The cards have gained a new popularity in the last few years as a number of mobile phone applications allow people to do their own readings at a click of a button.

JAMES WARRENDER

AUTOMATIC WRITING

"Writing said to be produced by a spiritual, occult, or subconscious agency rather than by the conscious intention of the writer."

Automatic Writing is a form of psychic ability where through trance a spirit can use the sitter's body to write freely. Hippolyte Taine, a French historian first reported cases of Automatic Writing in the third edition of his work "De Intelligence" in 1878. He researched and discovered a number of people who had witnessed the ability or had it happen themselves.

Automatic Writing became popular in the Victorian era, especially during séances or other meetings to contact the dead. During this time people would report that the spirit would take control of their body and write letters, poems or sometimes entire books. The parapsychologist William Fletcher Barett concluded that Automatic Writing would be more successful when used with a pencil and thin paper and conducted by one person while another group hold a séance.

Author, Arthur Conan Doyle studied Automatic Writing and wrote in his 1918 publication "The New Revelation" that Automatic Writing comes from an external spirit working through the writer's subconscious"

Fernando Pessoa, a Portuguese poet also had experiences with Automatic Writing. He claimed to have been taken over and felt "owned by something else" and had the experience of having his arm raised over his head without him doing so. He also reported seeing strong magnetic auras and having strong visions while carrying out

Automatic Writing.

Automatic Writing became very popular once again in the 1950s through to the 1970s when mediums such as Ethel Meyers, who most famously worked with Hans Holzer, was known to produce hundreds of pages of Automatic Writing. Sometimes she would even write on the walls of haunted locations if she didn't have paper.

The poet Robert Desnos was famous for his ability to use Automatic Writing. He claimed a number of his works were produced with the ability including his popular poem "Mourning for Mourning". The wife of the Irish author William Yeats also claimed to be able to use Automatic Writing.

One of the most notable cases of Automatic Writing comes from the author Jane Roberts (1929 – 1984). Roberts wrote the "Seth Material" over a period of twenty years between 1963 and 1983 with her husband. "Seth" was a spirit that was channeled by both Roberts and her husband, who would give insights into the spirit world, answer questions on life after death and give spiritual guidance to the couple.

They first contacted "Seth" in 1963 while conducting a Ouija Board session. Soon after, Roberts began to hear voices in her head that told her to use Automatic Writing. It was not long after this that "Seth" began to give out his information. Roberts had the works published and over the following twenty years she had 12 "Seth" books completed (only 10 of these were during her life time, the last two were published after her death).

Since Roberts died, many others have also claimed to have made contact with "Seth" and another 14 books have been published on his words of guidance since 1984.

Automatic Writing found a new lease of life with paranormal research teams who still utilize the ability in investigations today and many leave with some very interesting results.

PLANCHETTE

"A small board supported on castors, typically heart-shaped and fitted with a vertical pencil, used for automatic writing and in séances."

The planchette is a device used for Automatic Writing. It is different in the sense that it is used for a group of people to conduct an Automatic Writing session instead of just one person. The idea is for the sitters to place their hands on the planchette and it will move spelling out words or messages.

The term Planchette comes from the French for "little plank" It is often in a heart shape, on castors and has room for a pen or pencil. It became popular with the rise of the Spiritualism Movement and it appeared in its earliest form with letters of the alphabet placed around it, much like a Ouija Board.

Allan Kardec, the founder of Spiritism recorded the invention of the Planchette on 10th June 1853 while at a séance. One of the sitters at the séance had become bored of the normal séance techniques and results and decided upon himself to upturn a basket and place a pencil through it, allowing the group of people to conduct automatic writing together. It gave "astounding" results and Kardec quickly got to work on the idea, making it more secure and changing the basket for a bit of wood. The idea took off and made its way across the world.

Its widespread use across Europe saw the Bishop of Viviers rally against its use and wrote a pastoral letter in 1853 asking for them to be banned. Most people ignored this and the use of the Planchette grew within the realm of Spiritualism but not so much outside as the séance and the Ouija Board did.

The Planchette arrived in the USA in 1858 when two spiritualist friends Robert Dale Owen and Dr. H. F. Gardner returned from Paris with the device. It interested so many people that their friend G. W Cottrell manufactured the Planchette on a large scale the following year which went on sale across the country.

The device became more popular again in 1867 when a British publication "Once a Week" published an item on the use of the Planchette and how it was a gateway to "the other side". The article was reprinted throughout Europe and in America and reignited people's interest for the item. The company that produced the Planchette Kirkby & Co reported 200,000 were sold in their debut season alone.

With the increased popularity of Ouija Boards and Table Tipping, the Planchette took a more secondary role and had ceased production entirely by the 1940s and the wood used for their production was recycled during World War II.

Again, with the help of paranormal investigation teams in recent years, the Planchette has once again seen an increase its use, but sadly still not as popular as it was in the early days of its use.

DEMONIC POSSESSIONS

"Spirit possession is a paranormal or supernatural event in which it is said that animals, demons, extraterrestrials, gods, spirits, or other disincarnate entities take control of a human body."

Possession is found in just about every Religion and Culture in the world. It has its roots in pre-history and is found in Christianity, Islam, Judaism, Shamanism, Spiritualism and Wicca.

It is often seen as harmful to the person that it is happening too and can damage the spirit that is attempting to invade someone. The spirit is said to often be a malevolent being and someone who is going through a Possession could experience: forgetfulness and erased memories, fits and fainting, gaining access to hidden knowledge, changes in vocals or facial structure, the appearance of injuries, scratches or bite marks and sometimes even experiencing super human strength.

Possession is unlike channeling which a medium or psychic may do as they have no control over the possessing entity. Only when an exorcism is done by a Priest the entity will leave.

Among the earliest references to Possession comes from the Sumerian People who believed that illnesses and problems with the mind all came from demonic possession. They called their own Priests, or Sorcerers as they were known, to apply bandages to the affected person to trap the demon inside until it died.

Other early references to possession came in the form of the Cuneiform Tablets which contain prayers to certain Gods asking for protection from Demons.

In Shamanic Cultures, possession is also treated in the form of exorcism and a number of diseases are attributed to various demons which take the form of animals. While in Christianity, demons are known as the Devil in a lesser version of himself or as fallen angels. Exorcism is also said to rid someone of a possession in this religion too.

One of the most famous cases of possession in recent years is the story of Roland Doe. His possession and later exorcism inspired author William Peter Blatty to write "The Exorcist".

Roland Doe was the only child brought up in a German-American Protestant family. He was close to his Aunt Harriet, a spiritualist who encouraged him to play use a Ouija board. Not long after her death in January 1949, scratching noises started coming from the walls of the family home and even from within his mattress. His parents initially assumed it was mice, but when his bedroom furniture started moving around and objects such as fruit began sailing through the air, they soon began to worry.

It wasn't just at home this happened. At school, his desk began sliding across the floor and once injured another pupil. The boy often experienced blackouts, and started to become violent and would shout random words and phrases. In desperation, his parents now convinced he was possessed by his dead aunt turned to their Lutheran church minister. He referred them to the Catholic Church.

When a local priest visited, Roland screamed at him in perfect Latin, 'O sacerdos Christi tu scis me esse diabolum (O Priest of Christ, you know that I am the Devil).

The boy was admitted to the Georgetown University Hospital and a first attempt was made to exorcise him, but was abandoned after five nights when he slashed the senior priest down the arm with a bedspring.

Roland's parents then moved west to St Louis where they turned to another priest, Father Bowdern. By now Roland had an aversion to anything sacred and spoke in a guttural voice. He was moved to the psychiatric ward of the city's Catholic-run hospital.

It has been suggested that for years after, the Catholic Church banned the priests from speaking about what happened next, although author William Peter Blatty managed to unearth the details about the story for 'The Exorcist'. We will look at this further in the next chapter on Exorcists.

Thank you to Tom Leonard and those at strangemag.com for help researching this chapter.

EXORCISMS

"The expulsion or attempted expulsion of a supposed evil spirit from a person or place."

Much like Possession, Exorcism can be traced back through various Times, Cultures and Religions. Exorcisms are performed by causing an entity to swear an oath, performing an elaborate ritual or commanding it to leave in the name of a higher power.

They were requested and performed throughout the early ages, right through until the 18th Century which saw a steep decline in the number of Exorcisms. This lasted until later in the 20th Century where there were a 50% increase in numbers in the 1960s and 1970s, due to the high level of media attention they would get.

In the Catholic Religion, Exorcisms are performed in the name of Jesus Christ. These Exorcisms or "Major Exorcism" as they are known can only be performed by a priest with the permission of a bishop. There are also "prayers of deliverance" which anyone can say but act as more of a blessing than an exorcism.

There are guidelines for Major Exorcisms in Section 11 of the Rituale Romanum which guides priests on how to successfully perform an exorcism, when it may be required and how to check the possessed person isn't suffering from any form on psychological or physical illness before carrying it out.

The Exorcist, a consecrated priest will recite prayers according to the rubrics of the mass and may take use of religious symbols or materials to evoke God in the name of Jesus or Archangel Michael to intervene with the possession. Some possessions may take severely weekly exorcisms before a demon will fully disappear. Once the demon has been removed, the formally possessed person is not seen as evil or unholy or even seen as responsible for what happened.

There are three official rules that must be followed for an exorcism.

1. It must be done by a priest with the proper knowledge on how to perform it.

2. It must never be broadcast in the media. It should be treated with the utmost discretion.

3. More than one person must be present during it, preferably a family member.

This takes us back the case of Roland Doe who received an exorcism due to his demonic possession as detailed in the previous chapter. The whole truth of what the priests say they witnessed finally came out in 1978 after workmen demolishing part of the St Louis hospital found the official record of the exorcism. It detailed how night after night over four weeks, Father Bowdern performed the exorcism rite on Roland while a young, athletic priest, Father Halloran, held the writhing boy down.

Blotched writing, apparently in blood, would appear on Roland's skin, spelling out 'Hell' or 'Evil' or sometimes simply 'Hello', they said. Asked what he called himself, the boy once creepily replied, 'I will answer to the name of Spite.'

Then one night in April the boy suddenly cried out, 'Satan, I am St Michael! I command you to leave this body now!' Roland's body went into a final violent spasm and then he said, "He is gone!"

The boy never behaved oddly again. He disappeared from public sight and reportedly told the church he remembered nothing of what happened to him.

Thank you to Tom Leonard and those at strangemag.com for help researching this chapter.

PREMONITIONS

"A strong feeling that something is about to happen, especially something unpleasant."

Premonitions are a type of ESP which involves seeing into the future in the form of visions or dreams. There have been recorded cases of premonitions throughout time dating back thousands of years.

The most famous person to record his premonitions was Nostradamus (1503 – 1566) a French apothecary who became famous of his perditions, some of which have come true. Some of his most well known precisions include: the Great Fire of London (1666), The French Revolution (1789 – 1799), The rise of Hitler, The assassinations of JFK and RFK and the 9/11 Terrorist Attacks (2001). He has also predicted the end of world in the year 3797.

Over the last 100 years there has been a lot of time put into studies of premonitions. In recent years, these studies fall into two categories.

- Free Response Studies

These are experiments in any form of premonition or precognition through dreaming or other visions. Those who claim to have these premonitions are studied in sleep labs at the Maimonides Medical Centre and have produced some suggestive results but due to the complex nature of the experiments and high price for carrying them out, they are not done too often.

- Forced Choice Studies

These studies include the use of Zener Cards or other pictures where someone who claims to be able to experience predictions will be asked to use their ability to correctly establish what a card or picture will be. A parapsychologist Samuel G. Soal worked with various subjects and asked them to tell him what five animals appeared on cards he had especially made. This experiment showed promising results. These studies still continue today but are subject to people coming forward who can experience premonitions.

There have been a number of prominent cases of prominent throughout history, a small sample of them follow:

- Hilary Beachy, 1864

Hilary Beachy owned a hotel in Montana. His good friend Lloyd Magruder travelled upstate to sell $15,000 worth of goods to gold miners. On his way home Magruder was mugged by a group of four men. One of the men murdered him by hitting him with an axe. His body was hidden in the woods and the men made off with his goods.

Back at his hotel, Beachy had a dream that same night that he saw his friend being murdered but most importantly he saw the face of the murderer. A few days later the four men arrived at the hotel looking for a room. Beachy recognised the man from his dream and after a quick inspection of the men's belongings he found Magruder's saddle. The police were called and the men were arrested and later confessed to their crimes.

- John Raymond Godley, 1946

One night in 1946, Godley dreamed that he had the next day's newspaper and he saw the results of the horseracing. Upon waking he remembered the winner's name and placed a bet on it. It won.

Godley had a second dream not long after which detailed the winner of that day's Grand National. He once again placed a bet on the horse and it too one.

Over the next two years Godley would have another eight dreams detailing horse race winners. The dreams happened less and less often after 1947 and had disappeared entirely by 1958.

- Stephen Stolarski, 1950

In 1950, Stolarski had a dream that he was robbed. The following day he was held up at gun point and the robbers fled with the day's takings from his shop.

Two years later he had a similar dream and decided that he would place that days takings directing into the bank in the early evening. Just before closing three men came into the store and once again held him up at gun point. They fled when they discovered there was no money on the premises.

- Raphael Gonzales, 1981

Less than one week before he was murdered, the shop manager dreamed he would be killed by a former employee of the store. So shaken by this dream, Gonzales told the other employees.

The following week, the former employee from Gonzales dream robbed the store along with his brother, fired shots and killed Raphael before getting away with the money box. Soon after, one concerned employee told the police about Gonzales dream. The police, not too sure what to do interviewed the accused employee who broke down and confessed to his crime.

Premonitions are still popular today with books, websites and entire organisations set up to deal with them.

SPIRIT PHOTOGRAPHY

"A type of photography whose primary attempt is to capture images of ghosts and other spiritual entities."

With the invention of the camera, spirit photography became popular in the late 19th century. It was used by paranormal investigators and parapsychologists to attempt to catch the image of a ghost on camera.

One of the first people to attempt it was William H, Mumler in 1860. Mumler discovered the technique by accident when he developed a photo and found a second person in it that wasn't there when had taken the image. It turned out to be a double negative but the photographer began working as a medium, claiming to be able to get photos of people's loved ones to appear with them. He was eventually found out to be a fraud.

Despite this the popularity of spirit photography continued. Fred A. Hatton became an official Spirit Photographer working for various mediums and travelled the country showcasing what he had captured.

Arthur Conan Doyle and William Stanton Moses were also keen on the photography. It was Doyle who came up with the theory that it was in fact Ectoplasm that was being captured on camera.

Another famous Spirit Photographer was William Hope. He became well known for his "amazing" abilities to capture a spirit on camera. Harry Price, the famous paranormal investigator discovered Hope was also a fraud by marking his photographic plates so Price would know if the photos had been tampered with or not. Arthur Conan Doyle fought back at Price's claims and wrote "The Case for Spirit Photography" in a bid to clear Hope's name.

The most famous case of Spirit Photography is "The Brown Lady of Raynham Hall". In September 1936 Captain Hubert C. Prouland, a London based photographer and his assistant Indre Shira were visiting Raynham Hall in Norfolk to take photographs for an article that was to appear in "Country Life" Magazine later that year.

They had taken a photograph of the staircase already and were setting up for another when Shira saw a "vapour like form" that gradually took the shape of a woman which moved down the stairs towards them.

Shira quickly took the lens cap off from the camera and took the photo. Later when it was developed he found he had captured the now famous image of the lady. The image and their experience at the Hall was published in the December 26th 1936 edition of the magazine and it also made in into an 1937 edition of "Life" Magazine.

The negative was reviewed and tested at the time and showed no sign of any fowl play on the photographer's part. Today, skeptics believe that the men may have, knowingly or accidently had some grease on the lens of the camera which caused the ghostly woman to appear.

Interestingly, recently discovered documents in the Hall have told that residents in the house over 100 years prior to the photograph being taken had experienced the haunting of a lady. Two guests, on two separate occasions saw a lady walking the halls in a brown dress.

The woman hasn't been seen since 1936 but staff at the house, which is now a museum, say they have experienced strange events around the building that they put down to the Brown Lady.

The Brown Lady is said to be the ghost of Lady Dorothy Walpole, the sister of Robert Walpole, the man generally seen as the first Prime Minister of the United Kingdom. She was entrapped at the hall by her husband after he discovered she was having an affair. She stayed in the house until her death.

Today, paranormal investigators still use Spirit Photography and with the advancement in photography it is becoming a much more popular method of paranormal research.

JAMES WARRENDER

BANSHEES

"A female spirit whose wailing warns of a death in a house."

The Banshee is often seen as a mythical creature much like unicorns or fairies, but over the past 200 years they have been reported more and more, mainly in Ireland and in the Scottish Highlands. There are also reports found in early Norman history.

The Banshee is meant to appear most commonly to the families with a surname beginning with "O'" or "Mac" as well as many members of the Airle Clan. She was first reported as far back as 1380 in the publication of an article by Sean MacCraith. He reported his family hearing the "dreaded" scream and a few hours later his mother died.

One such family wrote a report on their Banshee named "Eeuul" who was the ruler of 25 other Banshees. She told the family that she would warn of death but they should listen out for the screams of multiple Banshees as this would signify the upcoming death of a noble person.

The Banshee is often seen wearing a white or gray dress with long pale hair which she may be seen combing. An Irish tradition says that if you see a comb on the street you should never pick it up as it belongs to a Banshee who is trying to lure in unsuspecting people to their deaths.

In the last three years there have been two reports of Banshees in the United States of America. One is said to walk around the Tar River in North Carolina which is a notorious spot for suicides. The Banshee will scream out every time someone jumps into the river.

The second sighting occurs in South Dakota. She is heard screaming but at no stage has anyone who has heard her screams died. Many believe she is in fact screaming about her own death as a woman was killed near the place she is heard to scream many years before.

TIME SLIP

"Where a person, or group of people, travel through time via unknown means"

Timeslip is perhaps one of the most intriguing areas of the paranormal. The phenomena occurs when someone or a group of people appear to travel through time and see a place as it once was, decades or even centuries before.

Due to the nature of these events it is difficult to trace back exactly where they were first reported from or even gain an insight into why they happen but in the last

150 years there have been a number of interesting documented cases of Timeslip.

One of the earliest recorded incidents happened to Charlotte Anne Moberly (1846–1937) and Eleanor Jourdain (1863–1924), two friends who were travelling in France together in 1901. They had decided to visit the Palace of Versailles as they were unfamiliar with it and the area so they took a train into Versailles. After touring the area they took a guidebook and began a walking tour where they soon became lost after missing a turning to take them to llée des Deux Trianons. With the help of their 1911 book on the incident "The Adventure" the rest of their story follows:

"The two women began walking up a dirt path where they saw an old, deserted farm house with a plough outside and a woman waving white cloth out of the window. They both reported a feeling of oppression and dreariness came over them. They then saw some men who looked like palace gardeners, who told them to go straight on. Moberly later described the men as "very dignified officials, dressed in long grayish green coats with small three-cornered hats." Jourdain noticed a cottage with a woman and a girl in the doorway. The woman was holding out a jug to the girl. Jourdain described it as a "tableau vivant", a living picture, much like Madame Tussauds waxworks. Moberly did not observe the cottage, but felt the atmosphere change. She wrote: "Everything suddenly looked unnatural, therefore unpleasant; even the trees seemed to become flat and lifeless, like wood worked in tapestry. There were no effects of light and shade, and no wind stirred the trees."

The Comte de Vaudreuil was later suggested as a candidate for the man with the marked face allegedly seen by Moberly and Jourdain.

They reached the edge of a wood, close to the Temple de l'Amour, and came across a man seated beside a garden kiosk, wearing a cloak and large shady hat. According to Moberly, his appearance was "most repulsive... its expression odious. His complexion was dark and rough." Jourdain noted "The man slowly turned his face, which was marked by smallpox; his complexion was very dark. The expression was evil and yet unseeing, and though I did not feel that he was looking particularly at us, I felt a repugnance to going past him. A man later described as "tall... with large dark eyes, and crisp curling black hair under a large sombrero hat" came up to them, and showed them the way to the Petit Trianon.

After crossing a bridge, they reached the gardens in front of the palace, and Moberly noticed a lady sketching on the grass who looked at them. She later described what she saw in great detail: the lady was wearing a light summer dress, on her head was a shady white hat, and she had lots of fair hair. Moberly thought she was a tourist at first, but the dress appeared to be old-fashioned. Moberly came to believe that the lady was Marie Antoinette.

After this, they were directed round to the entrance and joined a party of other visitors. After touring the house, they had tea at the Hotel des Reservoirs before returning to Jourdain's apartment.

They visited the Trianon gardens again on several occasions, but were unable to trace the path they took. Various landmarks such as the kiosk and the bridge were missing, and the grounds were full of people. Trying to come up with an explanation, they wondered if they had stumbled across a private party, or an event booked that day. However they found that nothing had been booked that afternoon. During their research, they thought they recognized the man by the kiosk as the Comte de Vaudreuil, a friend of Marie Antoinette, who herself had been thought to have been seen by Moberly." (The Adventure, 1911)

Another famous example is that of "The Vanishing Hotel" where the Simpson and the Gisby families were driving through France on their way to a holiday in Spain. They claimed to have stayed overnight at a "curiously old-fashioned hotel" and decided to break up their return journey at the same hotel but were unable to find it, despite returning to the very spot where the hotel stood. Photographs taken during their stay were missing, even from the negative strips when the pictures were developed.

More recent cases include a number of people experiencing a Timeslip on Bold Street in Liverpool as recently as 1996. Thank you to h2g2.com for this story:

"The following is a story from the mouth of a Merseyside Policeman who inadvertently travelled back in time when he was off-duty in July of 1996 in Liverpool City Centre's Bold Street area.

Frank, the policeman in question, and his wife, Carol, were in Liverpool one sunny Saturday afternoon shopping. At Central Station, the pair split up; Carol went to Dillon's Bookshop to buy a copy of Irvine Welsh's 'Trainspotting'. Frank went to HMV to look for a CD he wanted. Twenty minutes into his short stroll to the music shop, he walked up the incline near the Lyceum Post Office/Café building which leads onto Bold Street intending to meet up with his wife, when he suddenly noticed he had somehow entered an oasis of quietness.

Suddenly, a small box van that looked like something out of the 1950's sped across his path, honking its horn as it narrowly missed him. Frank noticed the name on the van's side. 'Caplan's'. When he looked down, the confused policeman looked at his shoes to see he was standing in the road. Frank crossed the road and saw that 'Dillon's Book Store' now had 'Cripps' over its entrances. More confused he looked in to see not books, but women's' handbags and shoes.

When he looked around, Frank realized people were dressed like those from the 1940's. Suddenly he spotted a young girl in her early 20's dressed in a lime coloured sleeveless top. The handbag she was carrying had a popular brand name on it, which reassured the policeman that maybe he was still partly in 19961. It was a Paradox2, but the policeman was slightly relieved, and he smiled at the girl as she walked past him and entered 'Cripps'.

As he followed her, the whole interior of the building completely changed in a flash to that of Dillon's Bookshop of 1996. As she was leaving 'Cripps', Frank lightly grasped the girls' arm to attract attention and said; 'Did you see that?' She replied; 'Yeah! I thought it was a clothes shop- I was going to look around, But it's a bookshop.'

It has been recently proved that 'Cripps' and 'Caplan's' were actual businesses based in Liverpool during the 1950's."

It seems clear based on these three cases that the characteristics of a Timeslip include the feeling of unreality but the ability to interact. Today Timeslip experiments are used by paranormal investigators. They recreating a scene that may help generate the emotions felt by the spirits when they were alive to help them communicate easier or to help create a full manifestation of a time slip.

PART II
FAMOUS GHOSTS
&
THEIR HUNTERS

THE ENFIELD POLTERGEIST

The Enfield Poltergeist is one of the most well documented cases of a poltergeist in modern times. It happened in the Harper Household in Enfield, London, starting in August 1977.

Mother, Peggy Harper became worried one evening when two of her four children, Janet and Peter complained that there were loud knocking noises coming from the walls of their bedroom. She first thought the children were making up the claims but upon investigation she heard the knocks as well. They eventually died down.

The following night, the children made the same complaint to their mother, but this time they were more frightened as their beds were jolting up and down and "going all funny". They also heard the sound of someone shuffling about as if they were wearing slippers, but only when the lights were switched off. As soon as they were switched on the sounds stopped.

The knocks suddenly started up again one night and while investigating the bedroom, a heavy chest of drawers slid eighteen inches across the floor. Peggy pushed them back, but as soon as she did they slid out again but this time she couldn't push them back. Worried, she noticed a light on in the neighbour's house so she went across to them for help.

The neighbours came and examined the house but found no one or no cause to explain the activity, but they did hear the knocking on the walls. They decided to call the police who came and did a search of the house and also found nothing. A police woman did see a chair slide across the floor. She later signed a statement confirming what she saw.

Over the following couple of days the haunting got worse. Small plastic bricks and marbles would be thrown across rooms and when they landed they were found to be hot, far too hot to even be held. Once again the police were sent for along with a local medium and two journalists from a newspaper.

The journalists stayed in the house for hours and nothing happened. It was only when they were leaving did the flying bricks continue – bombarding the reporters. It was them that called on the help of Maurice Grosse, a leading member of The Society of Psychical Research.

Grosse arrived at the house exactly one week after the hauntings began and kept in close contact with the family and held nightly vigils. It seemed to go very quiet for a short while until September 8th when a loud crash was heard from Janet's bedroom. A bedside chair had been thrown across the room, landing on its side. As the vigil was coming to an end, no one was prepared for it, but they set a second vigil in the bedroom and captured the chair on camera moving a again.

Later that night, marbles were thrown, doors started opening and shutting of their own accord and there would be sudden breezes in the house that came from no where. The haunting and investigation by Grosse made front page news on September 10th, 1977 and it was picked up by a local radio station that held a two hour live programme about it which featured Grosse and Peggy.

The haunting continued with the inclusion of interference with electrical items in the house and mechanical failure, including the cameras and infrared cameras brought in by the BBC. Tape recorders and audio recorders also failed.

The haunting continued over the next two years, as did Grosse's investigation. He noted that the poltergeist continued to move drawers, wrenching drawers from cabinets, pulling bed clothes off of beds, making strange puddles of water appear and starting small, contained fires.

It was around this time that a voice began to come from Janet's mouth. She had no control over the voice and was often seen to be in a trance state while speaking in the deep voice. She would speak for hours with this voice and it was discovered that the poltergeist was using her false cords to speak. Actors need special training to use their false cords and can only use them for a short period of time before any damage happens.

The voice said he was the ghost of a man named Bill who had died of a brain haemorrhage while sitting in an arm chair in the house many years earlier. Grosse believed that Bill could communicate with the raps and asked how long ago he stayed in the house. 53 knocks followed.

After this revelation, the haunting got worse still. Janet was famously captured on photograph being thrown out of bed by the ghost and one evening a reported challenged the entity to see what it could do. A bed was slammed up against the bedroom door and Janet levitated several feet in the air, which was witnessed by people passing outside.

Grosse came to the conclusion that Janet was the focus of the haunting and called in doctors and psychiatrists to examine Janet to see if she was really experiencing something unexplained or if there was a medical condition. After six weeks of investigation, the medics could find no problems with Janet and they also reported that there was no damage done to Janet's voice – which there should have been by using the false cords.

The haunting began to die down by September 1979 and by the end of the year peace had returned to the house and Grosse and the journalists left. The ghost was never heard from again. In a strange twist, three years later in 1982 a letter arrived at the house addressed to Peggy. It was from a man claiming that his father, William Wilkins, known as Bill, had lived and died in the house after suffering a brain haemorrhage.

The case has gone down in history for its activity and results. It has inspired many books, documentaries and films, perhaps most notoriously the BBC1 Screen One special "Ghostwatch" on Halloween 1992.

JAMES WARRENDER

THE SAN PEDRO HAUNTING

During the Summer of 1989 a woman got in contact with American paranormal investigator and parapsychologist Dr. Barry Taff telling him that his neighbour, Jackie Hernandez had been having some bad experiences with ghosts in her San Pedro home. Jackie didn't want to contact Taff herself as she put the experiences down to stress. She had recently given birth to her second child but was estranged from her husband. A few months later, Jackie made contact with Taff herself.

She told Taff that on a number of occasions she had seen the full apparition of a man sitting on her children's bed and at her dining table. She also reported hearing muffled voices, loud banging coming from her attic and water "pouring" out of the walls.

The claims of the haunting interested Taff so he, Barry Conrad, a camera man and director and Jeff Wheatcraft, a photographer descended on the small bungalow to investigate. Taff noted that upon arrival at the house they found Jackie to be in a state of high anxiety and depression.

The men were also met with a smell that they described as "rotten organic matter", a feeling of over pressure, and the sound of a "200 pound rat thumping about the attic". Jackie went on to tell the investigators that she had witnessed items such as lamps, children's toys and chairs had been thrown about. Cans of juice were also thrown at her which would hit her. She spoke of the man that she had seen as in his 50s or 60s with sunken, emancipated looks and wearing a checked shirt.

Before they left that evening, Wheatcraft and Conrad ventured into the attic to take some photographs. Not long after they entered the attic, Wheatcraft's camera was pulled from his hands. The shock of the incident caused the two men to make a quick exit from the attic. A few moments later, after composing themselves, they returned to the attic where they found that Wheatcraft's camera had been split in two and placed at different corners of the attic. Wheatcraft went to collect the pieces of the camera but before he got there he was pushed, by what he later described as a "bony hand" which sent him crashing into the rafters and requiring medical attention. The investigators left the house soon after.

A few days later, on September 4th 1989 Jackie called Conrad at midnight in a state of distress begging him and Wheatcraft to come to the house because the activity was happening. She had awoken in the night choking on a dark mist. Upon the investigators arrival Conrad began to notice a series of strange lights flying around on the view finder of his camera. These were leading up to the attic.

They were about to enter the attic when Jackie's neighbour called the men back to the living room where there was a strange red liquid dripping from one of the cabinets. This fluid was later analysed and was found to be human, male blood with heavy iodine and copper levels.

The investigators then once again made their way to the attic. While setting the ladder up for the men, Jackie was shocked when the hatch was pulled out of her hands. While discussing what had happened they were all interrupted when there were three loud snapping sounds, as if someone was clicking their fingers. Wasting no more time the men made their way up to the attic, a move that Jeff Wheatcraft would never forget.

Wheatcraft and Conrad were discussing what had happened last time they were there but were cut short when Wheatcraft shouted out and was pulled backwards. Having the only source of light in a camera flash, Conrad took photographs to see what had happened. He found that Wheatcraft had had something placed round his neck which had been pulled up over a nail sticking out from one of the rafters, hanging him.

Conrad fought to get Wheatcraft down and succeeded. He helped him down the hatch were he was met by Jackie and her neighbour. While calming him down they noticed that Wheatcraft had a plastic clothes line tied round his neck. Later examinations found that line had been tied in a sea man knot. Wheatcraft declined to return to the house ever again after that night.

For a short while afterwards, Conrad and Taff continued the investigation in Jackie's house. They witnessed the dark mist that had choked Jackie and experienced a strange evening where the smoke detectors in the house would beep in answer to their questions. This became stranger when they discovered that there was no power source getting to the detectors.

Jackie moved out of the house in October of that year, hoping that it would bring an end to the haunting but sadly for Jackie that wasn't to be. Almost instantly she began to experience strange events in her new house. Most worryingly of all, while moving a television from the shed into the house, Jackie and two of her new neighbours witnessed the same man Jackie had seen before appear on the television screen. She invited Conrad and Wheatcraft back to investigate.

The investigators came to Jackie's new house and put it under surveillance. They set up a number of cameras around the property but found that one camera in particular would never work and when it did they would discover it had been rotated to face away from where it was originally looking, the shed.

One evening, the group decided to experiment with the Ouija Board in the house. During the session they made contact with a man who said he was born in

1902 and was murdered in 1930 by a friend who was trying to take his wife from him. He gave his name as Herman and was murdered by being pushed into San Pedro Bay. He lived in what later became Jackie's home. He also gave the message "phantoms fill the skies around you."

The spirit then began spelling out "Jeff" and explained that Wheatcraft looked like the person that had killed him and he hated Jeff for that. The chairs and tables began to shake and Wheatcraft was picked up and thrown across the room. He hit the wall and then the floor with such force the others initially thought he was dead.

This, along with the events in the attic caused Jeff to enter a deep depression and suffer from Post Traumatic Stress Disorder, something he has only recently recovered from.

Not long after these events, Jackie returned to San Pedro to visit her family and decided to stay in a motel. One evening she reported a ball of light which lead her out of her motel room and to a local cemetery and to the grave of Herman Hendrickson. Jackie ran back to her motel where she discovered that the walls were gratified in red lipstick with the words "Mad" and "Angry".

Jackie told this occurrence to Conrad who searched through the San Pedro News Paper archives and was shocked to discover that the report of Herman's death was in a paper dated March 25, 1930 but it had been ruled as an accident, not murder. Something that Conrad believed this was why Herman's spirit was angry.

Jackie once again moved hoping that this time the haunting would subside, she was wrong. Instantly she experienced movement of books, furniture and other appliances, but she reported it didn't feel as threatening as before.

While Jackie seemed to be experiencing less, Conrad and Wheatcraft, who shared a flat, were experiencing much more. The spirit of Herman had attached itself to the men and would not leave them alone.

Their gas cooker would turn itself on and ignite. There would be times they would find pieces of paper, books or other flammable objects placed onto a lit ring. Once they were shocked to find a box of bullets, which were normally kept in a cupboard, placed on the cooker.

They once returned from filming to find their window had been smashed, they cleaned up the glass and took it to the outside rubbish bins. When Conrad went back up stairs to his flat he was shocked to find a piece of the glass which he had just taken outside was placed on his typewriter which could have cut him. They also reported furniture moving, bottles floating in the kitchen, lamps and books would be pilled on top of each other and knifes would be thrown around the house.

Most worryingly of all, both Wheatcraft and Conrad would wake up in the night to find open pairs of scissors under their pillows. Wheatcraft once awoke to find a pair stabbed through the pillow next to him. The haunting seemed to come to a stop after one evening when Wheatcraft was cut by the entity.

The haunting seemed to die down soon after this and Wheatcraft, Conrad, Taff and Jackie all went their separate ways, but the ghost of Herman Hendrickson was never too far away.

In the early 1990s Barry Conrad was speaking to his housecleaner. It was no secret that Conrad had a fascination of ghosts, although it wasn't well known that he was involved in the San Pedro haunting. Naturally their topic of conversation soon turned to the paranormal.

The housecleaner told Conrad that she had once seen a ghost. It was during the Summer of 1989 and she saw an old man "in his 50s with a sunken face and he was wearing a checked shirt." Slightly worried, Conrad asked the housecleaner where she was staying when she saw this ghost. Her replied haunted him. "In my house near San Pedro Bay". It seemed the ghost of Herman Hendrickson was terrorising all of San Pedro, not just Jackie.

Hendrickson hasn't been reported for a number of years now but Jackie still says she feels his presence from time to time.

JAMES WARRENDER

THE BELL WITCH

The Bell Witch was a case which originated in Tennessee from 1817 and was experienced by the Bell Family. It is the only case in history where the death of a man has been blamed on a ghost.

John, his wife Lucy and their two children John Jr. and Betsy lived on a large farm land in an area called Red River which would later become Adams, Tennessee. In 1816 they wished to extend their land to the field behind their home. John asked the neighbour, a woman named Kate Batts, who many said was a witch, if she would sell the land to him. She agreed but during the process she and John began a bitter disagreement over just how much of her land she would sell.

She claimed that John had taken too much and had paid too little for it, but the courts didn't listen. When they were leaving court Kate stopped John and told him she would make it her duty to haunt the family for what they had done to her, witnesses claimed she was "hell bent" on carrying out her threats.

The Bell Family received word just a few days later that Kate had died. That very night, John Bell was returning home when he saw when he described as a "half dog, half rabbit" animal in one of the corn fields. He shot at it and thought nothing more of it until that evening when the family began to hear knocking noises in the house. The noises got so loud and intense that John would run outside when they began to try and catch someone doing it. He never did.

The haunting continued and got worse, they began to hear the whispered voice of an old lady singing and a few days later they were sure it was the ghost of Kate Batts. Once they had identified her she began to make physical contact by pinching the family, stabbing them with needles and throwing items around the kitchen. She also began to scream at the family.

Betsy got the brunt of the haunting. Batts would slap her, push her over and attack her, sometimes without warning. John also experienced her a lot more and was reported to have been both physically and mentally tortured by the Witch. The family could go no where without Kate tormenting them.

The reports of the haunting became well known that people would travel from as far as 100 miles away to attempt to see or witness The Bell Witch. The case also grabbed the attention of General Andrew Jackson, who would go on to become the 7th President of America. He and three men travelled to Tennessee to witness the ghost. As they approached the Farm, their horses stopped moving. Jackson is reported to have said "By the eternal boys, it is the witch". Seconds later the Witch's voice was heard shouting "All right General, let the wagon move on, I'll see you later tonight." The horses then started to move again.

One of the men with Jackson claimed to be a "witch tamer." Having been at the house for a few hours, the "witch tamer" pulled out a gun and claimed the witch was scared to do anything as he had a silver bullet in the gun that would kill any evil spirits. He joked that the witch couldn't do anything.

Immediately, the man screamed and began jerking his body in different directions, complaining that he was being struck with pins and beaten severely. The men left soon after and never returned. The haunting continued for the next few years.

In December 1820, John Bell became ill. He had been experiencing difficulty breathing and moving for almost year after the attacks from the witch. He was left confined in the family home. Any attempt he made to leave was stopped by the witch who would slap him to the ground and remove his shoes.

John fell into a coma on December 19th and died the following day. Immediately after his death the family found a strange bottle next to his bed. They gave it to the cat which instantly died. Seconds later the Witch's voice was heard screaming out "I gave Ol' John a big dose of that last night, which fixed him!" John Jr. threw the bottle into the fire which exploded sending a strange light up the chimney.

Bell's funeral was well attended but the mourners were plagued by Kate Betts. Her voice was heard all over the town boasting about killing John. She later began singing. Her voice didn't stop until the last person left his grave side. The Bell Witch left soon after many believing that as she had succeeded in killing John, her work was done.

The entity returned in 1821 and told Lucy Bell that she would return seven years later. Batts kept her promise and returned briefly to haunt John Bell Jr. But her visitations seemed much calmer and she discussed "the origin of life, civilizations, Christianity, and the need for a mass spiritual reawakening" She also warned of the upcoming Civil War. Before she left she promised to return to visit Bell's family 107 years later.

The most direct descendant of Bell at that time in 1935 was Dr. Charles Bailey Bell. Dr. Bell wrote a book about the "Bell Witch," published in 1934. He never made reference to any visitations from the Witch and he died in 1945.

Even today the Bell Witch is reported to still haunt the area where the farm house stood but she is in a more relaxed state now. Often manifesting herself in the form of candle light or laughter.

Many argue that the story is a simple urban legend but the haunting was first recorded in a book about the history of Tennessee in 1886, 60 years after the death of John Bell. The book reports:

"A remarkable occurrence, which attracted wide-spread interest, was connected with the family of John Bell, who settled near what is now Adams Station about 1804. So great was the excitement that people came from hundreds of miles around to witness the manifestations of what was popularly known as the "Bell Witch." This witch was supposed to be some spiritual being having the voice and attributes of a woman. It was invisible to the eye, yet it would hold conversation and even shake hands with certain individuals. The feats it performed were wonderful and seemingly designed to annoy the family. It would take the sugar from the bowls, spill the milk, take the quilts from the beds, slap and pinch the children, and then laugh at the discomfort of its victims. At first it was supposed to be a good spirit, but its subsequent acts, together with the curses with which it supplemented its remarks, proved the contrary"

The haunting became popular again in 1894 with the publication of Martin Van Buren Ingram's book "An Authenticated History of the Bell Witch" which was based on the diaries of John Bell Jr.

THE BERINI HAUNTING

In the late 1970s, Joe Berini (a name given to protect the family's identity) moved his family made up of his wife, Rose and their two children into Joe's ancestral New England home. On their very first night in the house, the family first experienced the haunting. The voice of a little girl was heard. At first she was heard crying but later in the night she spoke to Rose, telling her "Mama, Mama this is Serena". No one in the family knew of any girl with that name.

A few days later their daughter Daisy was having an operation to have her tonsils removed due to complications her heart stopped on the operating table. She did survive but the timing of Daisy's health scare and the appearance of Serena didn't go unnoticed. The apparition also coincided with Joe's Grandmother suffering and eventually dying from a stroke. Joe also awoke one evening to find Rose choking in her sleep. When he managed to wake her up she said she had suffered a nightmare where she had been strangled by her ex-husband.

After these events and from Christmas 1979 onwards the haunting seemed to have fallen quiet. Without warning in March 1981 Rose saw the ghost of a young boy dressed in white walking along the upstairs landing. She explained that seeing the apparition was like "looking through a milk bottle". She went on to explain that the ghost walked around for nearly two hours. The boy appeared again a week and a half later and spoke to Rose. He asked her "Where do all the lonely people go? Where do I belong?"

The following day Joe saw the young boy walking in and out of each bedroom of the house "as if he was looking for something". After spending a long while in each of the rooms the young boy found a spot on the floor and sat there for the entire night. In the morning when he realised the boy had gone, Joe pulled up the floor boards around where the boy was sitting and found a medallion of the Virgin Mary.

The young boy would appear quite a lot to the family over the next while and on one occasion he told Rose that "My oldest brother is the only one that can help me". No one really knew what that meant but it was a turning point in the haunting. Things soon turned nasty.

The terror began soon after with objects flying around the house in an unpredictable manor, the phone would get pulled from the people's hand, doors would slam shut of their own accord and the ghost seemed to pick on Rose.

A local priest came to help the family who told them the best thing to do would be to ignore the ghost. So the next time the small boy appeared Rose carried on as if he wasn't there. This may have been a bad idea as she heard loud footsteps and a window slammed shut so hard it smashed.

They returned to the church for more help who sent a priest to bless the house and it did seem like a successful blessing... for a short time anyway.

In June 1981 a new entity arrived in the house, an entity that the family described had come "straight from hell". He was a sinister hunched back male who would only wear black, had a long cape and had large feet and a gruff voice. The ghost told the family "I am a Minister of God" but his behaviour which was made up of intimidation and fury made the family believe he had nothing to do with any God.

The entity injured Rose one day by slamming a door in her face. He would also distract her while she was praying by pulling at her Rosaries and making obscene comments towards her. All the family were struck by objects that he had thrown which included a lamp which smashed over Rose. It was also capable of over moving furniture and one day it slammed the retractable stairs into the loft so hard, the roof cracked. The family also reported that any, if not all of their religious symbols in their home either disappeared or would be found broken.

On another occasion Rose had her arm pulled so hard up behind her back that she couldn't breathe. She would often awake to find herself levitating above her bed and be pulled down to the ground. She would also discover large bruises on her skin.

The entity became its most violent two months later. Joe had gone into work late one evening and after he had left Rose witnessed the bedroom walls shake. The bed levitated and the door slammed shut. In a panic, Rose ran to the children's bedroom but as she got there, their doors were slammed shut and she was dragged by an unseen force back to her room where it began to cut and choke her.

She managed to break away and phone Joe who came right home. When he got there he found that the bed was levitating two feet off of the ground and Rose was huddled in the corner of the room clutching a crucifix.

Despite all that had happened to them the family refused to leave the house. This was until one morning a few weeks later Joe discovered a large, heavy carving knife had been stabbed into the kitchen table. Fearing for their lives the family left while and exorcism was held.

They returned four weeks later and Joe decided to return the medallion of the Virgin Mary to where he found it in the floor boards. The house fell calm and silent after this. The Society of Psychical Research spent a few evenings at the house after the exorcism and reported that "whatever bad had been in the house is now gone".

THE AMITYVILLE HORROR

It is perhaps the most notorious haunted house in the entire world. Anyone can identify it with just a photograph of its iconic windows and even now with a changed address many still flock to 112 Ocean Avenue to see the house that inspired 'The Amityville Horror'.

Many sources suggest that the house in question was once owned by 'John Ketcham' a notorious witch who fled Salem during the infamous witch trials of 1662 – 1663 and continued to practice black magic in the house. These claims are false. In fact, a quick look through the house's history will tell you it was formally the site of farmland before being sold and the house was built in 1925 by John and Catherine Moynahan.

After they died, their daughter Eileen moved in with her family for a number of years until 1960 when the Riley family bought the house. They lived there for a time before selling the house to the DeFeo family.

The DeFeo family were made up of Ronald DeFeo Sr. (43), Louise DeFeo (42) and their children, Ronald Jr. (23), Dawn (18), Allison (13), Marc (12) and John Matthew (9). The DeFeo children grew up in the house while the younger children had spent their entire lives there.

Their home wasn't a happy one. Family patriarch, Ronald Sr. was physically abusive, often beating Louise, Dawn and the other younger children. Many nights would be spent arguing which would often continue into fights. Eldest son, Ronald "Butch" Jr. would often find himself with his Father's shot gun pointed at his head.

The fighting became too much for everyone and on November 13, 1974 while the family slept, Butch awoke at 3.15am, picked up his Father's gun and killed his entire family.

The police were called in the early hours of the morning where Butch was arrested for the murders. During his trial he claimed to have been possessed by a demon (some sources say it was an angry Indian Chief) and it was during this possession he killed his family. Butch was later given six sentences of 25 years to life. Each of his appeals has been denied.

The Amityville house stood empty for the next 13 months, the reputation it had stopped many potential buyers before they even entered the house. This was until December 1975 when newlyweds George and Kathy Lutz purchased the house for a mere $80,000. They moved in on December 19th with Kathy's three children from her previous marriage, Daniel, Christopher and Missy.

As soon as they arrived at the house, the Lutz Family began to experience strange occurrences, so much so that they called in the local Priest, Father Ralph J. Pecoraro to bless it. On his arrival at the house, Father Pecoraro began his blessing and while flicking holy water in the master bedroom when he heard a loud masculine voice shout "get out". Father Pecoraro quickly left the house and later that evening he called to tell the Lutz Family exactly what had happened to him and to warn them to stay out of a particular room (which was to become Kathy's sewing room) but his call was oddly disconnected to static. The Priest also experienced strange stigmata like blisters after his visit to the house.

Over the course of the next few days, the Lutz Family were continually plagued by a ever growing list of paranormal occurrences.

These included:

- Often waking at 3.15am, George would make his way to the boathouse. It was discovered that not only was this the time of the DeFeo killings, but Butch DeFeo is also said to have wondered to the boathouse to reflect on what he had just done.
- Even though they had moved in during the winter, the house was plagued by flies which would cover entire windows before disappearing as if they were never really there.
- Kathy had vivid nightmares about the DeFeo murders and was able to correctly identify in which order they were murdered and in which rooms.
- She would also report the feeling of being "embraced" by an unseen force in a loving and caring manor.
- While working in the basement, George discovered the "Red Room". A small room behind shelving that didn't appear in any blue prints of the house. The family dog would never enter it, but stand by it growling.
- Cold spots, odours of perfume and later excrement would be experienced in areas of the house

with no pipes or wind flow to explain it.
- George and Kathy saw the image of a demon burned into soot of the fireplace
- Their daughter Missy developed an imaginary friend named Jodie who appeared in the form of a "demonic pig like creature" with red glowing eyes.
- George would wake to the sound of the front door slamming. He would run downstairs to confront any potential intruder only to find the door locked and the dog sleeping undisturbed.
- Other noises such as the sound of a "Marching band tuning up" were also heard in the house.
- While researching the history of the house, the George discovered he held a strong resemblance to Butch DeFeo and later began drinking at The Witches Brew, a place where Butch often drank.
- Kathy would see glowing red eyes in the window of Missy's bedroom.
- While in bed, Kathy would "often" levitate up to two feet in the air before coming crashing down.

- Locks, doors and windows were damaged by an unseen force.
- Cloven hoof prints which were attributed to a "giant pig" appeared in the snow outside the house on January 1st 1976.
- A crucifix in the living room would rotate upside down and give off a sour smell.
- George would find teeth marks on his legs.
- George would often see Kathy transform into a "90 year old woman"
- After trying to carry out their own blessing of the house, they heard a voice telling them to "Please stop"

All these events took place within 27 days and on the 28th day the family fled, leaving all their belongings behind. Not a single member of the Lutz family has ever discussed what happened on that final night, deeming it too frightening to relive.

Twenty days after the family left, paranormal investigators Ed and Lorraine Warren entered the house to conduct a paranormal investigation with a local television station. During the night, Ed was pushed to a floor by a strong force and Lorraine was overwhelmed by a demonic presence. She also sensed the spirits of the DeFeo family covered in white sheets unable to leave the house.

In a 2013 interview Lorraine Warren stated that she still has nightmares about the Amityville House and that she would never return there again.

The Amityville Horror case has a lot of publicity due to the Lutz family selling their story and it became 'The Amityville Horror' by Jay Ansen. The story later became the 1979 film 'The Amityville Horror' and spawned a further 9 sequels between 1982 and 2012. In early 2013, Daniel Lutz returned to the house for a documentary where he recounted what happened in the house.

Whether it be an elaborate hoax or genuine haunting, it is safe to say that the Amityville Horror is one of the most frightening cases in paranormal history.

HARRY PRICE

Harry Price (1881 – 1948) was a British paranormal investigator. He is best known for his extensive and well publicised investigation of Borley Rectory in the 1930s and his work at exposing fraudulent mediums.

Price became interested in the paranormal at a young age after reading a number of ghost stories in newspapers. He trained as a stage magician for a number of years and his vast knowledge of conjuring and slight of hand allowed him to tell if any mediums were using trickery. His knowledge was so far advanced he was asked to join the Society of Psychical Research in 1920 where he specialised in exposing mediums.

He later joined the Magic Circle in 1922. While Price concentrated on fraudulent mediums he made it no secret that he believed that many were genuine.

After six years with the Society for Psychical Research, Price left after several clashed with the management, mainly over the Mediumship abilities of Rudi Schneider. The SPR were convinced that Schneider was a genuine Medium but Price had photographic evidence of him freeing his arm during a séance and manipulating objects in the room. Not willing to work with the SPR any more, Price left and set up his own investigation group, the National Laboratory of Psychical Research.

In 1934, Price would make an offer to the University of London which would see him fund, equip and manage a department for Psychical Research. The University agreed which saw the birth of The University of London's Council for Psychical Research. The organisation held all of Price's collection of books, investigation equipment and research.

During his career as a paranormal investigator Price was involved in a number of well known and well documented cases including:

Eileen Garrett

In October 1930, medium Eileen Garret made contact with the spirit of Herbert Carmichael Irwin who had died only a few days before on the R101 Airship Disaster over France. Garret had claimed that she was actually attempting to communicate with Arthur Conan Doyle at the time when Irwin came to her. During a number of séances Garret seemed to get answers from Irwin about the ship that no one, except those who had built the ship could have known. The sprit of Irwin even told her the faults that had happened which caused the crash. She also spoke with a number of other victims of the crash. Price was far from convinced about Garrett's claims and after a short investigation he discovered she had access to the blueprints of the airship as well as a crew list in her possession.

Brocken Experiment

In 1932, Price travelled to Germany to take part in a unique Black Magic experiment. He had been told that a particular Shaman in the area could successfully turn a goat into a boy. Price explained that he only took part in the experiment to convince everyone involved that it wouldn't work. Price was right.

Borley Rectory

Price's most famous case is Borley Rectory. The house was nicknamed "the most haunted house in England" Price published a book on the haunting in 1940 after investigating it for nearly a decade and living there on his own between 1937 and 1938.

As far back as 1863 people reported hearing footsteps coming from the house. In 1900 the rector's four daughters all witnessed the ghost of a nun at twilight walking forty yards from the front door of the house. They tried to talk to the Nun but as they got closer to her, she disappeared. They witnessed her on more than one occasion and people living near by and people in the house all reported seeing a phantom coach being driven by a headless horseman over a forty year period.

A new family, the Smiths moved into the house in 1928. While clearing out cupboards they found a small paper package which contained the skull of a young woman. This discovery led to an influx of activity. They would hear the servants bells ringing even thought they had been disconnected years before, footsteps would be heard coming from parts of the house that no one was in and the Smith family also had an experience with the phantom carriage.

Price first visited the house on 12th June 1929. He had been in the building for only a few seconds when stones were thrown at him and a vase smashed at his feet. During his first vigil he heard tapping sounds coming from inside the frame of a mirror.

Price was also called in by the next family to live there, the Foysters. Not long after they moved in they started experiencing stones and glass bottles being thrown, windows shattering and bells ringing. They also told Price that their daughter had been locked in a room with no key. The family tried their own exorcism but they were bombarded with stones. They left in 1935 after awaking one morning to find many walls in the house had been drawn on with undecipherable messages.

The house remained empty for a few years except from the odd visit from Price. He came to an agreement with the owner of the building that he could stay there until a new family could be found to move in. Price decided that the house should be put under 24 hour surveillance and hired a team of 48 people to stay in the with him on a rota to see what sprits they could find.

On the 27th March 1938, they decided to attempt a planchette séance where they made contact with a young Nun who called herself Marie Lairre. She had travelled to England from France so she could marry but she was killed in the former Rectory that stood on the site of the current one. She told them that her body was buried in the cellar and the writing on the walls had been her trying to get help.

Another more angry spirit called Sunex Amures told Price that he would set fire to the hall at 9pm that evening and that "the bones of a murdered person would appear"

Almost a year later on 27th February 1939 the new owner was unpacking his belongings out of boxes when he witnessed an oil lamp get pushed over. This caused the house to go up in flames and it burned to the ground. When the house was on fire many of the locals witnessed a ghostly Nun standing in one of the upstairs windows. An investigation into the fire concluded that it was started deliberately.

Price returned to the house where he took photographs of the burned remains of the house. When he had them developed, Price was shocked to see that one of his photographs had captured a brick flying in mid air. He returned to the site and dug through the remains of Borley Rectory where the brick was captured flying. Digging down to the cellar he discovered human bones. He told the local priest who had the bones buried in consecrated grounds.

Price became known across the world for his work at Borley Rectory and didn't work on another as famous case again until his death in 1948 from a heart attack. The rest of Price's archives were taken to the University of London from the time of his death until 1978 where the collection of more that 13000 books, press cuttings, photographs and reports remain today.

HANS HOLZER

Hans Holzer (1920 – 2009) was an Austrian born paranormal investigator he is best known for his research and investigations into The Amityville Horror house.

Holzer's interest in the paranormal began at a young age after being told ghost stories from his Uncle Henry. Holzer went on to study archaeology and ancient history at the University of Vienna but due to the threat of War his family left Austria for New York in late 1938. Holzer went on to study Japanese at the University of Colombia and obtained a PHD in Parapsychology which he went on to teach at the New York Institute of Technology.

His career as a paranormal investigator soon took off as he began working with a number of well known mediums including Ethel Johnson Meyers, Sybil Leek and Marisha Anderson. He is noted as the person who coined the phrase "The Other Side" which he called the paranormal.

He believed that ghosts could be divided into three separate categories:

- Ghosts

The imprint left in the environment that could be picked up by a sensitive person.

- Spirits

An intelligent being that could interact with the living.

- Stay Behinds

Those found to be earth bound after death.

Holzer made front page news in the UK when he investigated a reported sighting of the ghost of Nell Gwynn at her former London home. The house had been turned into a nightclub. Holzer met with a number of people that claimed to have seen the ghost of Gwynn walking around the building.

One member of staff had accidently been locked in one evening. She walked around the entire building looking for a way out. She tried the front door a number of times and when she went to try a third time she saw the ghost of Nell standing by it. She didn't feel frightened and walked up the doors which were now unlocked.

Holzer was fascinated by this story and spent the night in the building with some members of staff. During the night they experienced the strong smell of oranges, which many attributed to Gwynn as she had once been an orange seller. They also witnessed technical equipment failures and the lift would move between floors on its own. This could only have worked if someone pressed a button to operate the life which was in a locked room.

Holzer's most famous investigation was of The Amityville Horror house. He entered the house in January 1977 with medium Ethel Johnson Meyers. Meyers had no knowledge of the house seconds after entering the building she said "Who ever lives here will be the victim of much fierceness."

Meyers went on to claim that the house was built on a Native American burial Ground and the angry spirit of a Shinnecock Indian Chief named Rolling Thunder was active in the building. She went as far as to say that Rolling Thunder had possessed Ronald DeFeo Jr. and caused him to kill all of his family.

During the course of the investigation, Holzer took a number of photographs which on closer inspection revealed small halo like lights which hovered over bullet holes in the walls from the DeFeo killings.

Holzer caught a number of other strange lights and mists on camera in the house and on one photograph in particular he captured the image of four ghostly Indian spirits. Ethel Johnson Meyers went on to claim that she felt Ronald DeFeo Jr. and his family were chosen by the spirits to be killed because of their weakness. They wanted to show they were angry at a house being built on their sacred land. She also said that because Ronald Jr. was the weakest, he was chosen to be the murderer.

Holzer carried out a Ouija Board session in the house with Ethel Johnson Meyers and they were told that the spirits of the Native Americans would stay in the house but remain inactive "for some time" because they were happy that they got their message out there. The spirits of the DeFeo Family would also remain in the house but they wouldn't be active as they didn't want to frighten anyone.

Holzer wrote numerous books about his time in the Amityville House and also about the paranormal in general. In fact by the late 1990s he had over 150 books released on the paranormal and has gained a large following due to his knowledge of ghosts, spirits and stay behinds.

THE WARRENS

Ed Warren (1926 – 2006) and his wife Lorraine Warren (1927 -) were American paranormal investigators, best known for their cases which often involved demonic hauntings and their work with their own Occult Museum.

Ed Warren was a World War II Navy Veteran and former police officer who became a self taught demonologist, author and lecturer. Lorraine Warren was a clairvoyant and light trance medium. Their love for the paranormal lead them, in 1952 to launch the New England Society of Psychical Research which allowed them to investigate cases around America.

The couple had a vast collection of objects which they had collected from various houses, hotels and other places they had visited to investigate. The objects were linked to the case and were often the cause of the haunting. Ed would take the items, have them blessed and place them on display in an extension he had built onto his house. For a long time the collection remained private but it soon became the Warren's Occult Museum. Where members of the public could come and see the haunted objects for themselves.

The museum contains items such as: a seven foot tall Satanic Icon, human skulls, African fertility symbols and perhaps most famously the possessed Annabelle Ragdoll which although is on display is locked away behind a glass cabinet as the last person to touch the doll promptly met his death later that day when his motorbike's steering locked causing him to crash head first into a lorry.

The Warrens investigated over 10000 cases of hauntings over their career which included ghosts, poltergeists, possessions and exorcisms. Some of their most famous cases include:

- Amityville

Ed and Lorraine were among the first people to enter the Amityville Horror house after the Lutz Family fled. Their investigation is well documented and resulted in Ed being knocked down by the evil forces in the house.

- The Demon Murder

In 1981, Arne Johnson was accused of killing his land lord. Not long before this, the Warrens had investigated a case of demonic possession in Arne's brother. Because of this, Arne decided to plead not guilty by reason of demonic possession. This plea was denied.

- The Werewolf

The Warrens helped in the exorcism of Bill Ramsey, a man who claimed he was possessed by a demon werewolf. He had bitten many people, in some cases severely injuring them.

- The Smurl Family

Jack and Janet Smurl called in The Warrens after they were plagued by strange sounds, smells and demonic apparitions. Ed and Lorraine blessed the house and cleared it of three ghosts and one demon which had sexually assaulted Janet.

- Stepney Cemetery

Ed spent a lot of time investigating the sighting of a Lady in White that haunted the local cemetery. He reported that she would be seen almost every month and investigations conduced where she wasn't seen would provide interesting EVP results. Ed is now buried in the same cemetery.

- The Haunting in Connecticut

The Warrens spent time in a house, which was formally a mortuary and they claimed they had encounters with a number of ghosts and demons there. The events of this case became the inspiration for the film The Haunting in Connecticut.

- Perron Farm

The Perron's family home was haunted y a witch who lived there in the 19th Century named Bathsheba Sherman. She cursed the land so all that lived there died. She and other demons haunted the family. They were finally removed by the Warrens. This case has recently been made into the film The Conjuring.

- Annabelle Ragdoll

Of all the cases the Warrens investigated, the Annabelle Ragdoll is perhaps their most famous. The case follows Donna, a student living in a flat with her friend Angie in 1970. Donna received the Ragdoll from her Mum as gift.

No one thought the Doll was anything special but soon noticed that it moved on its own, very subtly at first which the girls put down to the doll being knocked or pushed in the passing. As time passed the doll moved more and more. She would be left on the end of Donna's bed and in the morning she would be found on the sofa.

A friend of the girls, Lou, hated the doll and thought it was bad. The girls laughed at him for thinking this. They soon began to change their minds when they would find bits of parchment paper lying around the house with the words "help us" written on them. This was made more bizarre as no one in the house had parchment paper.

One day, Donna returned home and found that the doll had blood, or red liquid coming from its hands. This prompted her to call in a medium. The medium told the girls that block of flats they stayed in was built on the site of a field where many years before a young girl named Annabelle Higgins had been found dead. Annabelle's spirit had remained in the area and when Donna took home the doll, Annabelle's spirit latched onto it. Thinking that this was innocent and quite nice, the girls allowed the doll to stay.

Lou began to have dreams about the doll where it would try and kill him. The girls continued to laugh it off. This was until one evening they were having dinner and they all heard a loud thud coming from Donna's room. They went to investigate, fearing a break in but discovered that there was nothing out of place except the doll which had been on the bed but was now in the middle of the floor. While Lou was picking up the doll to put back on the bed, his chest was slashed. He knew that the doll had been responsible and was amazed to find that within two days the deep cuts had healed. This is when they called in the Warrens.

After conducting an investigation of the house and the doll, Ed and Lorraine both agreed that the doll had been latched onto by a demon that had disguised itself as a young girl. They brought in a priest to exorcise the house, which became quite peaceful almost immediately and the Warrens agreed to take the doll home to their museum.

Both Ed and Lorraine agreed that they should take the B roads home as they didn't wish to be on the highway with the doll in case it messed with the car, which it did. In the short journey the engine, brakes and power steering all failed. Ed stopped the car and sprinkled the doll with holy water which stopped any interference long enough to get home.

While the doll was in the Warren's home it would be seen to levitate, appear in different rooms, move about and cause a great deal of fear to the couple. A priest was called to exorcise the doll but he laughed off the idea and on his way home his breaks failed, causing him to have a nasty accident. He survived and returned to the Warren's house a few weeks later to perform the exorcism. The doll was locked in a glass box which is held inside another display cabinet and hasn't bothered the Warren's since.

The Warrens continued to investigate the paranormal together until Ed's death in 2006. Lorraine continues to investigate new cases as she said Ed has told her through automatic writing to continue. She also continues to run the Occult Museum, but won't let anyone touch the Annabelle Ragdoll.

JAMES WARRENDER

SARAH WINCHESTER

As far as hauntings go there is nothing more odd and frightening than the story of Sarah Winchester and the Winchester Mystery House. Some could argue that the story of Mrs Winchester is more bizarre than any of the ghost stories associated with the house today. This is her story.

Many claim that some families are cursed. If you believe that then the Winchester Family are certainly are. Sarah was born in September 1839 in New Haven, Connecticut to parents Leonard Pardee and Sarah W. Burns. Not much is known about her young life, but what is known is that she married William Wirt Winchester, the son of Oliver Winchester of the Winchester Repeating Arms Company, when she was 23 years of age on September 30 1862. Many sources suggest it was a lavish wedding despite the fact that the American Civil War was in full force at the time.

After their wedding, Sarah became a well known social entity and would attend events, parties and gatherings all around town. As the Civil War continued, Sarah's wealth continued to grow as William and his Father, Oliver were given many Government contracts for Guns to use during the War.

Sarah's happiness continued in early July 1866 when she had a daughter, Annie. For the next few weeks, Sarah was very happy indeed. But sadly Sarah's happiness didn't last long. Annie developed Marasmus, a chronic malnutrition and wasting disease which slowly took her life. She died on 24 July 1866 at just a few weeks old.

After the death of her daughter, Sarah became very ill, both physically and mentally and in some ways never recovered from the shock of losing her daughter. She spent the next 15 years as a recluse. Only leaving her home to visit psychics and mediums and to attend a weekly Séance.

In December 1880 tragedy struck her family again when William's Father, Oliver suddenly died at the age of 70. William inherited the entire Winchester Repeating Arms Company and all of its assets. Sarah still felt bothered and confided in her husband that "bad things happen in a set of three" With the death of her daughter and her Father-in-Law it is said she couldn't relax and spent a lot of time panicking and waiting for something bad to happen. Her hunch was right. Sadly just three months after his Father's death. William Wirt Winchester contracted and died from Tuberculosis.

It is true to say that Sarah was distraught at the death of her husband. She was thrown into a spiral of depression which many say she never came out of. Upon the death of William, Sarah inherited the entire Winchester Fortune which at the time was $20,000,000 (In today's money that would have been $468,655,173). She would also inherit a daily income of $1000 from the company (That would be $23,432 every day by 2014's standards!).

Fearing that her family was cursed and that she would be next to lose her life because of it, Sarah began consulting a number of mediums. She was already fascinated by mediums and would visit them to see if any of them could contact her deceased daughter. On one particular day, Sarah visited a Boston based Medium who told her that her family were indeed cursed by the ghosts of all the souls killed by the Winchester Rifles. The only way for her to survive the curse would be to travel west and build a home for her and the spirits.

That is exactly what Sarah did. In 1884 she packed up and moved to California where she bought a six bedroom farmhouse from a Mr. John Hamm and instantly began adding and building to the house. Each night Sarah would hold a Séance in her Séance room where she would ask the spirits what she should build the following day. She would write down all the plans on tablecloths and hand them to builders the next day, she never drew up blueprints.

Sarah used her $20,000,000 inheritance to keep builders working 24 hours a day, 7 days a week to ensure the spirits were kept happy. But what no one expected was that Sarah's house would keep growing and growing. Stairways would twist and turn into walls. Windows would lead to doors which lead to 30 foot drops, there were rooms within rooms within rooms, cupboards that opened up into bathrooms. The building continued until the house became a complete labyrinth of corridors and rooms. Just what Sarah wanted. The medium told her that if she made the house confusing, the angry spirits would never find her.

By December 1905 the house had over 600 rooms spread over 7 floors and included an impressive tower. The 1906 San Francisco Earthquake destroyed the tower and the top three floors of the house. Sarah was trapped in her bedroom for a number of hours after the earthquake and felt that this was a sign from the spirits to stop working on the front of the house and the higher floors and begin to build outwards. She agreed to what the spirits wanted.

Sarah was obsessed with the number 13 and there are a number of examples of this throughout the house. There are 13 bathrooms, 13 panels of glass on many windows, 13 hooks for the 13 cloaks she wore to her nightly Séance and her final Will contained 13 sections which she signed 13 times. The majority of her belongings were left to her niece Marion M Marriott ('M' being the 13th letter of the alphabet).

Sarah continued to have work done on the house for a further 16 years after the earthquake. Work finally stopped on the house after 38 continuous years on September 22nd 1922 when Sarah died at the age of 82.

Today the house still stands and features around 40 bedrooms, 6 kitchens, 2 ballrooms, 13 bathrooms, 47 fireplaces (many with no smoke outlets) 40 flights of stairs, 2,000 doors and 10,000 windows. The house still holds her unique easy rise staircase which she built to make climbing stairs easier with her arthritis.

After Sarah's death workman began removing the furniture that she had left for her niece. It took 8 truckloads each day for six and a half weeks to remove everything that was allowed to go from the house and by February 1923 the house was open to the public and the first tourists began to visit. Sarah didn't allow visitors while she stayed in the house. In fact she once fired a worker for simply catching a glimpse of her face.

In 1924, Harry Houdini visited the house. It is said that he experienced something so terrifying within the building he fled and never came back. Did he see Sarah Winchester?

Houdini wasn't the first person to experience something frightening in the house and he certainly wasn't the last. Today the Winchester Mystery House is regarded as one of the most haunted houses in, not just the USA, but the entire world. Sarah's master bedroom has had an amazing 100 reported paranormal sightings, while her Séance room has had a massive 55. Many members of the public will report smelling freshly made chicken soup in the long since used kitchen areas. While others will see steam rising as if a boiling pot is on the cooker. The Hayloft is said to be haunted by two men who had a massive fight resulting in one man's death. Could they be arguing over the $3 pay that Sarah gave them each day?

Tour guides will hear their names being called out along empty corridors and a number of staff and tourists have spotted some of Sarah's workmen walking along the corridors still working to build the already completed house.

A fog in the shape of people can sometimes be seen floating around the house while books which once belonged to Sarah which are out on display will turn pages on their own. A large organ in the house will be heard playing itself and many of the doors can be heard banging during the night and many people will report seeing dancing balls of light and experiencing cold spots around the vast building. Most excitingly of all, Sarah herself has been seen walking around the house that she built and loved.

As you can see the Winchester Mystery House is an active location to visit and has certainly well earned its reputation as one of the most haunted houses in the world. But was Sarah really troubled by ghosts of victims of the Winchester Rifles or was she just a traumatised lady deceived into building one of the most impressive mansions the world has ever seen?

FOX SISTERS

The Fox Sisters, Leah (1814 – 1890), Margaret (1833 – 1893) and Kate (1837 – 1892) were successful mediums and paranormal researchers. They are perhaps best known for experiencing a haunting which lead to the birth of Spiritualism and the Spiritualist Movement.

The three sisters lived with their Father, John and their Mother, Margaret in Hydesville, New York – just twenty miles from Rochester. The house the family moved into was notoriously haunted with reports of rapping sounds and taps. The previous owner, Michael Weakman had fled the house due to the ghostly activity.

It wasn't long after the Fox Family had moved in that they began to experience the same hauntings. It frightened the younger sisters so much they shared a room with their parents. They searched all over the house for a logical explanation for the sounds but to no avail. On March 31st 1848, Kate made history. She asked the ghost to copy her as she snapped her fingers – it did.

What follows is an affidavit written by the sister's Mother a few days after they experienced the haunting and began to get answers from it:

"On the night of the first disturbance we all got up, lighted a candle and searched the entire house, the noises continuing during the time, and being heard near the same place. Although not very loud, it produced a jar of the bedsteads and chairs that could be felt when we were in bed. It was a tremendous motion, more than a sudden jar. We could feel the jar when standing on the floor. It continued on this night until we slept. I did not sleep until about twelve o'clock. On March 30th we were disturbed all night. The noises were heard in all parts of the house. My husband stationed himself outside of the door while I stood inside, and the knocks came on the door between us. We heard footsteps in the pantry, and walking downstairs; we could not rest, and I then concluded that the house must be haunted by some unhappy restless spirit. I had often heard of such things, but had never witnessed anything of the kind that I could not account for before.

On Friday night, March 31st, 1848, we concluded to go to bed early and not permit ourselves to be disturbed by the noises, but try and get a night's rest. My husband was here on all occasions, heard the noises, and helped search. It was very early when we went to bed on this night; hardly dark. I had been so broken of my rest I was almost sick. My husband had not gone to bed when we first heard the noises on this evening. I had just lain down. It commenced as usual. I knew it from all other noises I had ever heard before. The children, who slept in the other bed in the room, heard the rapping, and tried to make similar sounds by snapping their fingers.

"My youngest child, Cathie, said: 'Mr. Splitfoot, do as I do,' clapping her hands. The sound instantly followed her with the same number of raps. When she stopped, the sound ceased for a short time. Then Margaretta said, in sport, 'Now, do just as I do. Count one, two, three, four,' striking one hand against the other at the same time; and the raps came as before. She was afraid to repeat them. Then Cathie said in her childish simplicity, 'Oh, mother, I know what it is. Tomorrow is April-fool day, and it's somebody trying to fool us.'

"I then thought I could put a test that no one in the place could answer. I asked the noise to rap my different children's ages, successively. Instantly, each one of my children's ages was given correctly, pausing between them sufficiently long to individualize them until the seventh, at which a longer pause was made, and then three more emphatic raps were given, corresponding to the age of the little one that died, which was my youngest child.

"I then asked: 'Is this a human being that answers my questions so correctly?' There was no rap. I asked: 'Is it a spirit? If it is, make two raps.' Two sounds were given as soon as the request was made. I then said: 'If it was an injured spirit, make two raps,' which were instantly made, causing the house to tremble. I asked: 'Were you injured in this house?' The answer was given as before. 'Is the person living that injured you?' Answered by raps in the same manner. I ascertained by the same method that it was a man, aged thirty-one years, that he had been murdered in this house, and his remains were buried in the cellar; that his family consisted of a wife and five children, two sons and three daughters, all living at the time of his death, but that his wife had since died. I asked: 'Will you continue to rap if I call my neighbors that they may hear it too?' The raps were loud in the affirmative.

"My husband went and called in Mrs. Redfield, our nearest neighbor. She is a very candid woman. The girls were sitting up in bed clinging to each other and trembling with terror. I think I was as calm as I am now. Mrs. Redfield came immediately (this was about half-past seven), thinking she would have a laugh at the children. But when she saw them pale with fright, and nearly speechless, she was amazed, and believed there was something more serious than she had supposed. I asked a few questions for her, and was answered as before. He told her age exactly. She then called her husband, and the same questions were asked and answered.

"Then Mr. Redfield called in Mr. Duesler and wife, and several others. Mr. Duesler then called in Mr. and Mrs. Hyde, also Mr. and Mrs. Jewell. Mr. Duesler asked many questions, and received answers. I then named all the neighbors I could think of, and asked if any of them had injured him, and received no answer. Mr. Duesler then asked questions and received answers. He asked: 'Were you murdered?' Raps affirmative. 'Can your murderer be brought to justice?' No sound. 'Can he be punished by the law?' No answer. He then said: 'If your murderer cannot be punished by the law, manifest it by raps,' and the raps were made clearly and distinctly. In the same way, Mr. Duesler ascertained that he was murdered in the east bedroom about five years ago and that the murder was committed by a Mr. _____ on a Tuesday night at twelve o'clock; that he was murdered by having his throat cut with a butcher knife; that the body was taken down to the cellar; that it was not buried until the next night; that it was taken through the buttery, down the stairway, and that it was buried ten feet below the surface of the ground. It was also ascertained that he was murdered for his money, by raps affirmative.

"'How much was it - one hundred?' No rap. 'Was it two hundred?' etc., and when he mentioned five hundred the raps replied in the affirmative.

"Many called in who were fishing in the creek, and all heard the same questions and answers. Many remained in the house all night. I and my children left the house.

My husband remained in the house with Mr. Redfield all night. On the next Saturday the house was filled to overflowing. There were no sounds heard during the day, but they commenced again in the evening. It was said that there were over three hundred persons present at the time. On Sunday morning the noises were heard throughout the day by all who came to the house.

"On Saturday night, April 1st, they commenced digging in the cellar; they dug until they came to water, and then gave it up. The noise was not heard on Sunday evening nor during the night. Stephen B. Smith and wife (my daughter Marie), and my son David S. Fox and wife, slept in the room this night.

"I heard nothing since that time until yesterday. In the forenoon of yesterday there were several questions answered in the usual way by rapping. I have heard the noises several times today.

"I am not a believer in haunted houses or supernatural appearances. I am very sorry that there has been so much excitement about it. It has been a great deal of trouble to us. It was our misfortune to live here at this time; but I am willing and anxious that the truth should be known, and that a true statement should be made. I cannot account for these noises; all that I know is that they have been heard repeatedly, as I have stated. I have heard this rapping again this (Tuesday) morning, April 4. My children also heard it.

"I certify that the foregoing statement has been read to me, and that the same is true; and that I should be willing to take my oath that it is so, if necessary."

(Signed) MARGARET FOX, April 11, 1848.

- With thanks to the First Spiritual Temple for the transcript.

It was discovered after communicating with the ghost more, it was that of Charles B Rosna, a peddler who stayed at the house five years before the hauntings began. He had been murdered and buried in the cellar. The digging, mentioned in Mrs. Fox's affidavit, continued that Summer where a couple of human bones and hair were discovered.

It was over fifty years later that the full remains of the man were discovered as reported in a local news paper at the time:

"Rochester, N.Y., Nov. 22nd, 1904: The skeleton of the man supposed to have caused the rappings first heard by the Fox sisters in 1848 has been found in the walls of the house occupied by the sisters, and clears them from the only shadow of doubt held concerning their sincerity in the discovery of spirit communication.

"The Fox sisters declared they learned to communicate with the spirit of a man, and that he told them he had been murdered and buried in the cellar. Repeated excavations failed to locate the body and thus give proof positive of their story.

"The discovery was made by school-children playing in the cellar of the building in Hydesville known as the "Spook House," where the Fox sisters heard the wonderful rappings. William H. Hyde, a reputable citizen of Clyde, who owns the house, made an investigation and found an almost entire human skeleton between the earth and crumbling cellar walls, undoubtedly that of the wandering peddler who, it was claimed, was murdered in the east room of the house, and whose body was hidden in the cellar.

"Mr. Hyde has notified relatives of the Fox sisters, and the notice of the discovery will be sent to the National Order of Spiritualists, many of whom remember having made pilgrimage to the "Spook House," as it is commonly called. The finding of the bones practically corroborates the sworn statement made by Margaret Fox, April 11, 1848."

- With thanks to the First Spiritual Temple for the article

The haunting continued to get worse. Mrs. Fox's hair turned white through fear and the family had split up. Kate had gone to stay with her brother and Margaret went to stay with Leah who had moved to Rochester. The ghost followed the sisters to their new homes, with reports of the haunting getting worse. Leah and Margaret decided to experiment with the rappings, they called out the alphabet and asked the spirit to knock in response to the correct letter. They received this message:

"Dear Friends, you must proclaim this truth to the world. This is the dawning of a new era; you must not try to conceal it any longer. When you do your duty God will protect you and good spirits will watch over you."

- With thanks to the First Spiritual Temple for the message.

With this success, the sisters then decided to tour America giving public displays of the rapping in the form of a séance. Their publicity brought on the Spiritualism Movement which took America and Europe by storm.

The sisters also worked as mediums, passing on messages and conducting séances in front of audiences. Many sources indicate that Kate was the best Medium of the sisters. Along side the rappings, she also managed to produce spirit lights and full apparitions.

As their popularity grew, all the sisters suffered a serious drinking problem. This caused them all to, very publically, fall out. Margaret, angered by her sisters, gave an interview to the press where she said they had all been faking the rapping sounds all along. She later retracted this statement.

The Fox Sister never did regain their popularity after this incident and all three of them had died within the next five years. Their legacy still continues to this day, as most, if not all leading methods of spirit communication all derive from the Sisters and their investigations.

JAMES WARRENDER

PART III
HUNTING THE UNKNOWN

INTRODUCTION

As a "ghost hunter", something that I am often asked is how do you carry out a successful paranormal investigation? It is a very interesting process which takes a lot more planning that many people would think. Some would believe it is as simple as turning up at a haunted location, asking "is there anybody there?" a few times and coming home. If only it was that easy!

Over the following chapters I will guide you through what I believe are the steps that you need to consider and follow. We will look at: what you must consider before the investigation, how to carry out the historical research and the base line test.

We will then look at the investigation itself, the dos, don'ts and health and safety aspects of an investigation and the best ways to examine and distribute the results. I will finish by answering the question that I am asked more than any other in this field, "why do you ghost hunt in the dark?"

PRE-INVESTIGATION PLANNING

Before you arrive at your location and take part the investigation, you must take time to plan. It is the golden rule of pre-investigation, plan ahead, think ahead and time ahead.

In researching a location, it is best to chose somewhere that has had recent reports of hauntings. If you go to a location where once, in 1900, an entire household saw the ghost of a woman appear but she hasn't been seen since, you won't have much luck. Locations that have been reported haunted in the local press or through word of mouth from other investigators will have much better results.

That said, you must be careful as I have discovered in the past it is funny just how many new bars, nightclubs or tourist attractions which are just about to open seem to have a ghost. These locations must be thoroughly checked out first before you commit to any investigation just in they are looking for free advertising through your team.

My team and I would also warn others that you should avoid locations which are part of chains. These sites are more interested in making as much money as possible out of the group and will offer very little in return. One site asked our group for £1000 per room, per person, per hour – so access to the bathroom for a six hour investigation would be £30,000 alone! We felt in the end that these sites were actually trying to discourage paranormal groups from coming along, but instead of simply turning us down they would continue with E-mails back and forth until we were the ones to turn them down. Many other sites will point blank refuse, some will ignore you entirely while others will take the opportunity to not just say "no" but tell you how wrong paranormal investigation is and that we are all going to hell for it (This did happen to me once!).

While choosing the site, you also have to think about the logistics. Is it easy to get to? Does it have electricity? Is there a roof?

Once you are happy that you have chosen a location that will suit your team and yourself and that is happy for you to carry out an investigation there you must book it. In my group, we split the costs between us. Some sites are happy to pay the fees on the night of the investigation; others will want it up front. You must find this out before you book. If they are happy that you pay on the night, double check that all the team have the correct cash before arriving. I would also suggest you print out copies of any E-mails which confirm your plans and receipts of any payments made, simply to avoid any confusion on the night. Also take a note of the contact number for the location in case you will be late arriving or need to get in touch with them.

Once you have considered these factors, you can begin to plan else where. If the location is far away, you may wish to look into booking a hotel room or bed and breakfast for after the investigation if you or the driver doesn't wish to travel home at 5am. Our rule, as an Aberdeen based team is if we are further South than Dundee we will stay over after, if we are Dundee or closer we will consider coming home.

If you do decide to book a bed and breakfast, do remember to ask about a late check out if you wish to sleep in the following morning and if they will do a late breakfast as well. We also tend to ask if there are any other guests staying that night as we will be coming in sometimes after 4am and you really don't want to disturb other guests.

Before setting off remember to check and possibly print out directions from home to the hotel, the hotel to the location and the location to the hotel. You can never be too sure just how reliable a satellite navigation system can be, especially in the middle of no where. Remember to check your petrol as well. Will you have to stop on the journey and will you have enough to get you to the location?

Also check out the weather conditions before you leave. Not only will this keep you informed of driving conditions but it will give you an idea of how it will be during the investigation and for the journey home.

I will also urge you to ask the location management what their policy is on the use of Ouija boards, séances and calling out for spirit activity. Believe it or not we have organised an investigation, travelled across Scotland to get there only to be told we weren't allowed to do a Ouija board session or "do any of that calling out stuff" as the manager put it! It is also advised to ask where the location stands on the use of filming and photography equipment and the release of any footage or stills afterwards. Be sure to ask if the managers wish for the location to be named, I have been involved in an investigation where I wasn't allowed to reveal in print where we were going.

The last aspect to look into is your equipment. Make sure all your batteries are charged; have spares in case they run down and bring the mains charger as an extra back up. Make sure your torch works and that you have enough tapes to record on, or room on memory cards.

If you are happy that you have covered all of this, you can move onto the next stage.

HISTORICAL RESEARCH

Depending how well known the location is, it may be fairly easy to find out a lot of information about it or you could find that there is next to nothing known in the public domain.

To begin with I would suggest you go to your local library. You will be able to find a number of sources that can help you. I have found that members of staff at the libraries are more than happy to help, in the past I have been given access to books, archives and newspaper clippings which have proved very valuable to investigations

If possible I would avoid using the internet for research. It may be okay if you get information of the website of the location but I would be weary about other information that the internet has unless it is backed up. Although I do check out what is available online about the location, it may come up during the night and help identify people that have researched the building before arriving. I would urge you to check, double check and cross reference all information that you do get about the location.

In most cases you can speak with someone at the site who will give you as much or as little information you need. Some will also give you a brief overview on the night of the investigation. I would also suggest that if you can, try and cross reference the information given out at the site. There is one location that I have visited that has fed us false information to try and "catch out" the group.

It is a great idea to take a note of all the monarchs that reigned during the time the building was in use, right up to modern day. This can be a fascinating way to find out what times spirits may be from if you are using a Ouija board or using a medium.

I always try to research and take note of what hauntings are experienced in the building as well. The can be referenced in the final report if anything similar happens to your group. Tourist information shops will often have books or pamphlets on hauntings in the local area which are useful.

It is best to take a hard copy of all your notes on the night as you may not get access to a computer or internet access.

JAMES WARRENDER

THE BASELINE TEST

The baseline test is one of the most important aspects of paranormal investigation as this is what you will compare all your experiences and readings to during the night. If possible the baseline test is done a few days before an investigation but on the night of the investigation will work just as well.

To get the best overview you should take readings with an EMF Meter and K2 Meter of the rooms and check what mobile phone interference will do to the equipment within the environment. This will rule out any signal interference that may happen later on if someone forgets to switch their phone off. It is advised you take each of the readings twice. This will give you a firm reading.

Next you must look around the building, taking note of creaking floor boards, any natural drafts and any light that will come in from outside during the night. Take time to take a base reading of the ghost box and find out which local stations can be picked up in case they come through later on. Remember to check if your walkie-talkies work in the building.

Look around outside at what is around. Are you near a road? Could traffic sounds be heard inside? Are you near a bar or nightclub? Will the music or sounds of the party goers interfere with the investigation? Also attempt to find out if you are near a flight path and if members of the public can get access to the immediate area around the building. Taking note of the external temperature is important as it may effect the inside temperature. Knowing the moon phase can sometimes help as well.

Back inside you must take control photographs of rooms and log when you take them. This can be checked back later on if something changes or moves in the area. Record a couple of trial EVPs and listen back to what natural sounds are picked up on your recording device, this can rule out any interference on playback.

Also find out where the light switches are in rooms and ask if any of the lights or indeed anything else in the room is on a motion or time sensor. Investigate if the building has any central heating systems as this will affect the temperature readings. Also ask if the heating is on a timer and if so when will it come on and check out where the power sources are in the rooms.

Finally, getting a map of the layout of the location can be very valuable. Not only can you mark your finding from the baseline test on it, but it can be useful later on in the investigation, especially if a member of staff isn't on hand to direct you.

JAMES WARRENDER

THE INVESTIGATION

Begin your investigation with a group walk around with all the lights on. This will give everyone a chance to get use to the layout of the building and get a feel for it. Allow any mediums or psychics in the team to tell you what they are picking up and take a note of the equipment's readings.

Remember to have some form of audio or visual recording equipment with you at all times. Some groups will start with a séance before anything else to build the energy then move onto the walk around.

Once you are all satisfied with the lit walk around, it is time to switch the lights out. My group will then walk around the building again getting a feel for the location in the dark. It would now be advised to call out and attempt to get a reaction from the spirits at this stage.

Depending on what people feel and what is experienced it would then be a good time to split the group up into pairs or threes to investigate different parts of the building. Ensure that each group have a recording device, some form of equipment and a notebook. Remember to tell each other where you will be so you can rule out their movement.

After a while make sure you move the groups around. Try to cover as much ground as possible. You may be limited in time so if an area seems flat during a vigil, move on. You can always return at a later point in the night.

After a little while apart you may want to regroup to try a séance, Ouija board or table tipping session. My group will also attempt an EVP session and spirit photography session.

I urge you to just follow your instincts if you are drawn to an area, investigate it. If you are drawn to try an experiment, do it. Following your instincts sometimes provide amazing results.

That said I feel it is very important to do the following:

- Take as many photos as you can.

- Keep at least one EVP recorder (with a lapel microphone if possible) and one video recorder going at all times, even during breaks.

- Set up lock off cameras in the areas that are the most active.

- Keep notes at all times. I am bad for forgetting midway through the investigation!

- Keep the investigation running at all times if possible. If some of the group want a break that is fine but keep one or two people investigating. I have found that taking a break together will stop or slow down the energy and you may the find the building has become flat.

- Remember to factor in time to set up and pack up in the investigation. You have a lot of equipment that takes time to set up.

- Take note of where all your equipment is placed so you remember it at the end of the evening and so the group won't disturb it if it is locked off.

- Limit time for breaks

Remember, the golden rule is to cover as much ground as possible and attempt to get as much evidence as possible. You want to leave the building satisfied that you have the results you came to find.

THE DOS AND DON'TS

It may seem like the boring bit, but we will briefly look some of the rules that my group follow, I advice that you follow the same rules to keep everybody safe, secure and happy.

Do

- Follow the rules set out by the staff at the building.

- Ask prior to the investigation if the members of staff at the building are happy for you to carry out experiments.

- Treat the staff at the site with respect and

kindness; they are giving up their own time during the night for your investigation.

- Carry a torch at all times to safely move around between rooms in the dark.

- Carry identification in case you are asked for it.

- Take copies of E-mails confirming times and any receipts of payments with you.

- Arrive and leave at the times you have agreed.

- Bring your own refreshments unless you are told the site will provide for you.

- Always ask permission.

Don't

- Trespass or attempt to gain access to restricted areas.

- Drink alcohol prior to or during the investigation.

- Allow anyone to take part in the investigation under the influence of alcohol or drugs.

- Attempt to exorcise the spirits of the building or bless the area without prior permission.

- Touch, move or interfere with any displays, artwork or anything else in the location that you aren't allowed to.

- Help yourself to items in the gift shop or café.

- Make assumptions or believe that you are in charge.

JAMES WARRENDER

EXAMINING THE RESULTS

Once you have completed your investigation it is time to go through the footage, recordings and photographs you have collected.

The first stage of this process seems obvious but it is suggested that you digitalise all your recordings. Not just because this makes it much easier to view and play back, but it will back it all up if the devices fail.

As you go through the footage, take note of time codes of any anomalies or any other events that you wish to go over again. With the readily available editing software it is easy to edit the footage down to smaller clips. You will be able to change the contrast and put filters over the footage to get a better look at what you have captured. Many built in editing software to laptops and computers will do the job just fine.

As for the audio recordings, there is a lot of software which is free to download that will allow you to edit the EVP recordings and see the sound levels to attempt to work out what the sound could be.

With your notes it is advised that you put these into chronological order along with the readings from the baseline test and investigation to give a complete overview of the investigation. Remember to include any photos you wish to add, a full team list and a brief overview of the location and the history. Draw a conclusion based on your findings and include excerpts from interviews from members of your team that you may wish to include.

When it comes to sharing your evidence, we find it best to put it on the internet on our various social network pages. We will put up a full version of the report along with links to any videos or EVP recordings that we have uploaded onto video sharing sites. This will allow any people interested in the investigation to leave feed back and will allow you to take your investigations further.

If there is any interest from local press or media, precede with caution. Make sure you only do the interview if you know your investigation and group will be represented seriously without any silly puns or film references in their article or item. Also ask the press not to make the investigation sound more interesting that it was. We have had a simple investigation sound like a night in the Amityville Horror House in the past!

With all this in mind I hope that it gives you a clear outline on how to conduct a paranormal investigation which can be informative, safe and fun.

WHY GHOST HUNT IN THE DARK?

It is the one question I am asked more often than anything else. Lectures, talks and public investigations will always be stopped so someone can ask "Why do you ghost hunt in the dark?" Sometimes the question is phrased more like "If you want to see a ghost, but sit in the dark, doesn't this defeat the point?" or more rudely "Why don't you shut up, switch the lights on and go home?" Nice! Well, here are just a few reasons behind ghost hunting in the dark and during the night.

Powering Down

- Slowing and calming down is important to not confuse instruments such as EMF meters with anomalous readings. It also means less chance of air-conditioning/heaters causing drafts and hot spots, electronics going off and it gives the building a chance to settle.

No Light

- We're certainly not people with night vision ourselves, but using cameras that can read infrared (night vision) can help to bring out details in a spectrum of vision we don't possess. It's believed that in the infrared spectrum we might find something that has trouble showing itself in the human eye's range.

No Interference

- Without lots of cars on the road outside, children screaming in yards, telephones ringing, this is an ideal time to do a study. If you don't want to get confusing sounds and activity in your evidence files that can be explained by human intervention, then night time is your time.

Vision

- Admittedly, it's very easy to be distracted by wall hangings, items on shelves and light coming in from a window. With the lack of visual spectrum, like a blind person, hunters become keener with their other senses like smell, hearing, and bodily sensations of being touched and becoming cold.

Quiet Time

- Some ghost hunters believe that night time when things of a paranormal nature are most active. This is a time when homes and businesses are quiet, when if something of a spiritual nature is said to haunt the area, it could have the place to itself.

I hope this will shed some light (no pun intended) on this question. It is always something that I am glad to be asked and very glad to answer. There is method in our madness!

PART IV
HAUNTED LOCATIONS

TUTBURY CASTLE

There are traces of man living on the site of Tutbury Castle since as far back as the Stone Age but it wasn't until 1071 that the first version of the Castle was built. Twenty years later it was referenced in the Domesday Book and the first of many sieges upon the Castle took place in 1153 by Henry of Anjou – the later King Henry II. By 1175 he ordered the total destruction of the Castle.

Tutbury Castle was rebuilt in the late 12th or early 13th century, which also saw the building of a chapel known as St. Peter's. It was around this time that Henry III visited and stayed at the Castle before his son,

Lord Edward attacked it, causing severe damage.

In 1266, the Castle passed hands to Edmund Crouchback who would later become the First Earl of Lancaster. The Castle, from hereon throughout history would always belong to the Duchy of Lancaster who today is Queen Elizabeth II. Edmund soon began the restoration of Tutbury Castle and by 1298 it was 'firmly built and in substantial repair'

John of Gaunt inherited Tutbury Castle through marriage in 1313 and he began further repairs to the Castle and built the John Of Gaunt Gateway. Over the next 150 years, each owner added their own parts to the castle, which was then passed onto Margaret of Anjou, wife of Henry VI as part of their marriage settlement in 1449.

In 1511, Henry VIII visited the Castle and less than 50 years later it went under preparation to become a prison for Mary, Queen of Scots who would be held there four times between 1569 and 1585. During her time at the castle she was given her own home, known as 'Mary's Lodgings' Partial remains of her home can still be seen today.

Work continued on the castle up until 1647 when parliament, under the power of Oliver Cromwell ordered that it be demolished. Much of the castle was destroyed but what was left went under repair in 1660.

By 1725 reconstruction was complete and all surviving buildings from the various sieges over the years and newly completed buildings remain today.

The early 19th Century saw the Castle became a farm and the modern day kitchen and tea rooms were added on at that time as stables. There were plans to turn part of the castle into a prison in 1832 but the then Duchy rejected these plans.

1847 saw the first time tourists visited the castle and were allowed to tour the houses and various ruins. By 1952 it ceased to be a farm and over the next five years archaeological work rediscovered the remains of St. Peter's Chapel.

The Castle grounds remained open to the public but no access to interiors were allowed until 1999 when Tutbury Castle was leased to Lesley Smith who, after a lengthy restoration period, opened the entire Castle to the public for the very first time.

Tutbury Castle remains open to the public and more information can be found here www.tutburycastle.com

While Tutbury Castle has always held a reputation of being haunted, with some reported ghost sightings going back to the early 1900s, it wasn't until the Castle opened to the public in 2000 that the reports built up. Between 2000 and 2003 alone there were over 250 reported ghost sightings. One part of the castle, known as the King's Bedroom had to be closed to the public because so many strange events happened there.

Within the Great Hall and King's Bedroom a little girl has been seen wondering about, trying to grab the attention of visitors. A dark shadowy figure has also been seen in the rooms who chases people out because he isn't happy they are there.

Other ghosts including soldiers, hooded figures and wounded prisoners who have been witnessed walking around. Other visitors get a sense of danger and threat from some areas of the Castle.

One of the most famous ghost sightings at the castle is that of Mary Queen of Scots who is seen in the ruined remains of the South Range and walking the grounds.

Other Royal Ghosts reported is that of King Charles II who is seen in the Great Hall standing by the fireplace – he has been picked up by a number of different mediums as is King Henry VII whi is also seen in the Great Hall.

More recently, staff and visitors have seen and felt the presence of Oliver Cromwell, who seems to be unhappy that the Castle still stands. A portrait of him hangs in the King's Bedroom and it has been suggested that it has caused a recent surge of activity.

Tutbury Castle is certainly an interesting location and this author suggests you visit it as soon as you can!

With thanks to Lesley Smith at Tutbury Castle for her help with this chapter.

TOLBOOTH MUSEUM

The Tolbooth Museum was once Aberdeen's prison. It was built between 1616 and 1629 and is one of the oldest buildings in Aberdeen. The building which stands today, known as The Tolbooth is in fact the Wardhouse – the prison of the old Tolbooth Building. It is also known as the "High Tolbooth" or the "Mids O' Mar"

The prison opened in 1629 and was a place of great suffering and misery. Many people died within the walls, or spent their last night alive in the cells before being taken outside and hanged on Union Street.

At its peak, the Tolbooth had two busy periods. First during the later part of the

17th Century when Quakers were prosecuted in Aberdeen (and throughout the country as a whole) many were held in the Tolbooth. Some sources claim people were packed into the prison like "salmon in a barrel". It later became over crowded once again in 1746 after the Jacobites were defeated at Culloden. Over 150 prisoners were held in the building at this time.

One of the most famous prisoners of The Tolbooth is Peter Young who was a notorious gipsy and a gang leader who originated from Durrus. He and his family would hide out in an area called "Red Beard's Cave" and would lurk around attacking and robbing the locals. He and his wife, Jane Wilson would also rob people's homes. During a visit to Aberdeen, Peter and Jean attempted to rob a house but were caught. They were quickly locked up in the Tolbooth.

Peter was often allowed a lot of visitors while he was imprisoned. In fact he was allowed as many visitors as he wanted up to three times a day. Many would bring him gifts of wine and bread. Taking advantage of this, he used his outside contacts to smuggle in tools. These tools, hidden in wine bottles, allowed Peter to pick the lock of his and Jean's shackles as well as those of the other prisoners in jail. They then cut the bars of the window and managed to escape.

It is then said he made his way to Edinburgh and York where he continued his crime spree before being captured and brought back to Aberdeen where he was returned to the Tolbooth and was locked in a specially made iron cage that sat in the middle of the Condemned Cell. Peter was executed on July 2nd 1788 closely followed by Jean in August of that year.

The Tolbooth operated as a prison until 1809 when Bridewell Prison opened. The Bridewell was later replaced in 1831 by Aberdeen's more "modern" East Prison which served until Craiginches opened in 1891.

Once the Tolbooth closed it remained empty for a number of years before being used as storage for the City Council as well as wine storage but largely remained empty with quite a lot of the final prisoner's items left lying around the cells. Plans were put in place in the late 1980s to open the Prison as a Museum – this happened in 1995. Since opening to the public, the Tolbooth has had many reports of ghosts and hauntings.

Within a cell now known as the "Jacobite Cell" there have been strange sounds, like crying, reported. As well as a strange smell of honey, this is often smelled for long periods of time. Some could argue that this is Jacobite spirits as honey was used to treat their wounds after Culloden. A small "Great Escapes" Cell to the right of the "Jacobite Cell" is home to a sprit that likes to knock on the walks.

Downstairs in the slightly larger "Civic Room" and "Gaoler's Room" there is a poltergeist which likes to throw coins and marbles. It has also been known to knock over chairs and slam shut some of the large cell doors.

There is a particularly nasty spirit in the prison which makes people feel very uncomfortable. A number of mediums have suggested that he is a "faceless" prisoner unwilling to leave the last place he was held in before he died. He is known to change the atmosphere and make women cry. On a number of investigations women have been known to burst into tears or pass out within the lower cells of the building.

Other hauntings include that of a feminine voice calling out to visitors and investigators alike, she is even been known to call people's names. The apparition of an old man wearing a hat that walks around the first floor and is often associated with the time the building was used as a council storage.

Overall, the Tolbooth is a very active location but many, including myself, feel that the spirits are in visitation, they come and go when they please as sometimes an investigation of the prison can be quiet and peaceful while other times it can be like a war zone.

Out of my many, many investigations across the country I would say The Tolbooth Museum is one of the best places to experience the paranormal – but take a warning, not all of it is nice and you may get more than you bargained for.

BELGRAVE HALL

Belgrave Hall, situated in Leicester is said to be England's most haunted property. It has a rich history

The Hall was built by Edmund Cradock in 1709 as a home for him and his wife. Cradock was a wealthy hosiery merchant who wanted a large home of his own. Sadly Cradock didn't get much time to enjoy the house he had taken time to build as he died in 1713. His wife didn't want to live in the Hall after Edmund's death so she gave it up and it fell into the hands of the Leicester Trust.

Belgrave remained with the Trust for the following eight years until John and Helen

Simons purchased for their family home. Not much is known about the Simons family but the Hall remained with the family until 1845.

The Hall was purchased by John Ellis, who helped bring the railways into Leicester. He bought the Hall having plans not just for it to be the family home, but he also intended to run a hosiery business from it as well. After the death of John, the Hall stayed with the Ellis Family: first to his eldest son Richard, then down the line through John's seven daughters and their families.

Belgrave Hall finally left the Ellis Family in 1923 after the death of John's youngest daughter, Charlotte Ellis. She had no family and the Hall was put up for auction. It was bought by Thomas Morley.

Again, not much is known about Thomas Morley; however he left the house very suddenly one night in 1936 never giving an explanation but vowing never to return. Some say he was frightened by the ghosts of the Ellis Family or even Edmund Cradock who was annoyed that other people were living in his house.

Thomas Morley sold the Hall to Leicester Council for £10,500 in August 1936. Soon after, it became a museum, charting Leicester's History as well as the known history of the Hall itself.

It wasn't just Morley that experienced the ghosts of the house. It has been said that the Ellis Sisters too experienced the ghost of Edmund Cradock. They would often speak of a man walking on the upper landings that would try and frighten them. John Ellis would often laugh off such claims.

Ever since opening as museum more ghost sightings have been reported. Most famously is from 1998 when two ghostly white images were captured on the Hall's CCTV system. The figures which were seen in the gardens, hovering by a window nearly six feet off the ground have been nicknamed the White Ladies and many feel they are two of the Ellis Sisters coming back to check their beloved home.

A special investigation was undertaken by the ISPR Investigation Team in 1999 who invited Medium Derek Acorah to join them. Acorah and the team confirmed that there were a number of ghosts in the Hall including Charlotte Ellis and a number of children and servants still going about their daily business.

Today members of staff still encounter the ghosts with people reporting a woman in a Victorian style dress on the lower ground floor gazing out of the window. There are also sightings of a Green Lady and a Grey Lady walking the Hall at different times.

Other anomalies experienced include odd shadows catching people off guard and mysterious footsteps echoing through the Hall. Others also experience cooking odours which can include freshly baked bread or ginger bread, but there are no working kitchens on site.

One member of staff has recently said about the hall "Paranormal occurrences happen here on a weekly basis. We just become used to it."

RRS DISCOVERY

The Royal Research Ship Discovery was built especially for Antarctic expeditions and research in 1900 before launching on March 21 1901. It was the last traditional three mast wooden ship to be built in Britain and on it's maiden voyage to the Antarctic, the Discovery was captained by Robert Falcon Scott (1868 – 1912) and Ernest Shackleton (1874 – 1922).

The Antarctic Expedition lasted much longer than planned as Scott and his crew found the RRS Discovery was stuck in ice for over two years. It was only when a relief ship managed to find the ship that the Discovery and her crew were finally freed.

After Scott's voyage ended in September 1904 the ship was used as a Cargo Vessel which sailed from London to Hudson Bay in Canada until the outbreak of World War One when it was used to take weapons to Russia. In 1916 it was sent to save Ernest Shackleton from being marooned on Elephant Island. Following the end of World War One she was hired by various companies for Antarctic Expatiations.

In 1923 the Discovery was purchased by the Crown Agents for the Colonies and was given a complete renovation to be modernized to again be used for Antarctic research. It went on a further two expeditions between 1924 and 1931.

Upon her return in 1931, The Discovery was laid up until she was gifted to the Sea Scouts as a static training ship. Her engines and boilers were removed and used as scrap metal during World War Two.

Over the following few decades she began to fall into disrepair and was eventually gifted to the Dundee Heritage Trust in 1985 who put in a lot of time to restore the Discovery before opening her up as a Museum in 1986. She is currently docked in Dundee at the Discovery Point.

Since being gifted to Dundee Heritage, many on board the boat have experienced the paranormal. A number of people have heard footsteps walking around the ship. These ghostly footsteps are said to be that of Charles Bonner, a seaman who fell from the crows nest and died when he shattered his skull on the iron deckhouse.

Else where on the ship, a light bulb kept blowing above Shackleton's cabin. An electrician was called and no logical explanation could be found for the bulb's behaviour. Others have heard ghostly footsteps around the cabin rooms that are said to be that of Shackleton himself.

One of the more known ghost stories of the ship is of a member of the public on a tour of the Discovery stopped and spoke to one of the "guides" who was dressed up as a sailor from Captain Scott's time. After a lengthy conversation with the "guide", the person left and spoke to the staff about the very kind man downstairs dressed up as a sailor. The staff informed them that there was in fact no one working on the ship that day and in fact no one walking around dressed as a sailor.

The RRS Discovery is perhaps now more famous for its ghosts than its association with Captain Scott.

MARY KING'S CLOSE

Mary King's Close is an Old Edinburgh Close situated in the Old Town area of Edinburgh on the Royal Mile. It is made up of Mary King's Close and a number of other closes including Pearson's, Stewart's and Allen's. It is a well known haunted attraction in the town with a number of ghosts sighted.

The Close gained great notoriety when the Plague hit Edinburgh in 1645. It is said that worst hit area was Mary King's Close. The Council decided that the best thing to do would be to shut the gates of the close at both ends and leave the ill to die. A white cloth was tied over the gates to warn people not to enter. Some sources suggest that if someone was suspected of having the Plague, they would be lead to Mary King's Close where they would join the damned.

Not much is known the fate of those in the Close, but by 1685 the buildings were reoccupied. It was not long after this that the first reported hauntings began in the Close. George Sinclair who later became a Professor of Maths and Experimental Philosophy at Glasgow University, published the book "Satan's Invisible World Discovered; or, a choice Collection of Modern Relations, proving evidently against the Saducees and Atheists of this present Age, that there are Devils, Spirits, Witches, and Apparitions" Where he recounts one of the first ghost sightings in the Close:

"Mr Thomas Coltheart, a respectable law-agent, and his wife moved into a house in Mary King's Close. They took their maidservant with them, but she was so frightened by neighbours' reports that the house was haunted that she refused to remain there. One Sunday afternoon, shortly after moving in, Mrs Coltheart was sitting reading her bible when a ghastly apparition appeared before her – the disembodied head of a grey-bearded old man. Understandably, she fell into a swoon.

Later, she told her husband about it, but he put it down to her over active imagination.

However, that night, as they lay in bed, the ghostly head appeared to both of them.

They tried praying it away, but to no avail.

An hour or so later, a second apparition appeared: a young child, with a coat upon it, hanging near to the old man's head.

The child and the disembodied head hovered about the room for some time before being joined by a third apparition: a ghostly arm which seemed intent on shaking hands with the law-agent and his wife.

"In the name of the living God," cried Mr Coltheart, addressing the arm, "... tell me why thou troubles my family?

To my knowledge, I never wronged any man, by killing or cheating, but have lived innocently in the world. If thou has received any wrong, if I can right thee, I shall do my utmost for thee, but trouble me no more." But, despite the poor man's pleadings, things went from bad to worse. The bizarre phantoms were soon joined by a ghostdog, then a ghost-cat, and then a whole menagerie of spectral creatures. Before long, the floor was swarming with them.

Finally, as the terrified couple knelt on their beds praying for deliverance, they heard a dreadful groan and all of the apparitions simultaneously vanished.

Incredibly, the Colthearts refused to let these frightful events drive them from their new home. They lived out the remainder of their lives in Mary King's Close, and were not troubled again.

However, two later occupants, a harddrinking old pensioner and his wife, were startled one night to observe their candle start to burn blue. Shortly afterwards, the ghostly head re-appeared, and the terrified couple fled the house never to return."

It was from this point on the Close gained a reputation for being haunted.

In 1753 it was decided that the City Chambers (Then known as the Royal Exchange) was to be built on the site of Mary King's and the adjoining Closes. They were evacuated and some of the taller buildings were destroyed while the lower buildings were used as foundations for the Chambers that were about to be built.

The underground network of streets and houses remained hidden for over 200 years. The council who continued to own them occasionally would allow people down into the Close for unofficial tours. During this time it could be argued the visitors awoke the haunting that had stood undisturbed for so long. People would experience cold spots and strange scratching sounds around the various rooms.

In 1992 during a tour a Japanese Psychic Medium named Aiko Gibo senesced that there was a little girl named Annie who haunted one of the rooms. She was sad because she had lost her doll. Aiko immediately went out and bought her a little bear and left it in the room. Since the Close opened to the public in 2003, many tourists have continued this tradition by leaving a doll or bear for Annie in what is now called the "Shrine Room.

The hauntings still continue today with reports of tall, black figures walking figures walking the street, strange lights being reported on tours and odd apparitions being captured on camera.

The close is still a regular haunt for tourists and ghost hunters a like and many would still say that the previous residents haven't left and they still roam the streets living their daily lives unaware they are frightening and interacting with the living.

VALLEY OF THE KINGS

The Valley of the Kings, located on the west bank of the River Nile, is where for over 500 years the Pharaohs and noble Kings of Egypt were buried. It was in operation during the 18th through 20th Dynasties of Ancient Egypt.

Egyptologists can only guess at why this particular area was chosen for burials but many would suggest that it is due to the nearby mountain which takes the shape of a pyramid and the Ancient Egyptians felt the area to be one great, grand pyramid for the dead.

Currently, there are 63 confirmed tombs in the Valley while current excavations could find more. In recent years there have been a number of pre-burial chambers been discovered, but the exact number of tombs may never be known.

The Valley is the final resting place of a number of well known Pharaohs including Ramesses II, Tia'a and most famously Tutankhamen. While research has proven that the first Pharaoh to be buried there was Thutmose I after his 1493 BC death and the final King entombed there was Ramesses XI in 1078 or 1077 BC.

The Valley of the Kings is a very popular tourist attraction with over millions of tourists flooding in each year. It is fascinating to discover that tourists have been visiting the area since as early as 278 BC with Greek graffiti discovered, mainly in KV9, the final resting place of Ramesses V and Ramesses VI. The Valley was also visited by Napoleon in 1799 who took time to draw maps of the known Tombs. These maps are still used in modern research today. Work is still being done on the Valley and some suggest that as many as another one hundred tombs could still be buried underground.

With its long history and links to the dead, it will come as no surprise that the Valley of the Kings has a reputation for being haunted.

Many eyewitnesses have reported seeing a phantom Pharaoh riding a chariot drawn by black horses gliding through the Valley at midnight. No one can be sure of who exactly the Pharaoh is but some mediums have said it is a guard of the Valley keeping watch over the dead and making sure the Kings aren't disturbed.

Another well known ghost is that of Akhenaten, who ruled for 17 years and died in either 1336 BC or 1334 BC. He is noted for abandoning the traditional Egyptian polytheism and introducing worship centered on the Aten, which is sometimes described as monotheistic or henotheistic. Upon his death his successor Smenkhkare had him removed from history and asked three priests to curse his spirit to roam the deserts for all the afterlife. He is often seen by tourists and locals alike.

Watchmen at the Valley often report strange sounds including footsteps, clattering of wheels and angered screaming and shouting and a lot of shuffling in the entrance of the tombs.

Most famously the Valley is said to have a nasty curse. "Death shall come on swift wings to him who disturbs the peace of the King" was the warning on the door leading to where King Tutankhamen is entombed. It wasn't long before the archeologists who discovered the tomb began to die.

In late 1922, archaeologist Howard Carter had worked for seven years looking for King Tutankhamen's tomb in the Valley. Eventually, after digging down 4 meters beneath the Tomb of Rameses VI they found steps. After more digging the got to the twelfth step where they found a sealed stone doorway. Howard Carter immediately invited his financier, Lord Carnarvon to come to the site to be present for the opening of the tomb. On the 24 November, Carter and Carnarvon were present when all the rubble was removed to reveal the stone door with the seal of King

Tutankhamen in the plaster. It took another two days of hard work to clear another descending stairway full of rubble. This time they found a second door. The workers made a hole through the stone door and Carter looked in with the light of a candle. There was magnificent treasure in the room - and even more in the inner room, which took them another three months to get to. Lord Carnarvon himself opened this inner door on February 17th, 1923.

King Tutankhamen's mummified remains were inside three coffins. The outer two coffins were made of hammered gold fitted to wooden frames, while the innermost coffin was made of solid gold. The body was originally inspected by Howard Carter's team who cut up the mummy into various pieces: the arms and legs were detached, the torso cut in half and the head was severed. Hot knives were used to remove it from the golden mask to which it was cemented by resin.

It was only a few months later when Lord Carnarvon died on April 6, 1923. He was found dead at the Winter Palace Hotel. At 1:55 a.m. that day the lights in Cairo when he was meant to have died went out and plunged the people into darkness. Reportedly, at the same time, back at his home, his dog gave out a great howl and died.

King Tutankhamen's treasures went on exhibition to various museums around the world and Arthur C. Mace from the Metropolitan Museum of Art in New York and George Benedite of The Louvre in Paris each died after showing the treasures from the tomb.

The following is a list of other people possibly killed by the curse:

- Lord Carnarvon, financial backer of the excavation team who was present at the tomb's opening, died on 5 April 1923 after a mosquito bite became infected; he died 4 months and 7 days after the opening of the tomb.

- George Jay Gould I, a visitor to the tomb, died in the French Riviera on 16 May 1923 after he developed a fever following his visit

- Prince Ali Kamel Fahmy Bey of Egypt died 10 July 1923: shot dead by his wife.

Colonel The Hon. Aubrey Herbert, MP, Carnarvon's half-brother, became nearly blind and died on 26 September 1923 from blood poisoning related to a procedure intended to restore his eyesight.

- Sir Archibald Douglas-Reid, a radiologist who x-rayed Tutankhamen's mummy, died on 15 January 1924 from a mysterious illness.

- Sir Lee Stack, Governor-General of Sudan, died on 19 November 1924: assassinated while driving through Cairo.

- A. C. Mace, a member of Carter's excavation team, died in 1928 from arsenic poisoning.

- The Hon. Mervyn Herbert, Carnarvon's half brother and the aforementioned Aubrey Herbert's full brother, died on 26 May 1929, reportedly from "malarial pneumonia".

- Captain The Hon. Richard Bethell, Carter's personal secretary, died on 15 November 1929: found smothered in his bed.

- Richard Luttrell Pilkington Bethell, 3rd Baron Westbury, father of the above, died on 20 February 1930; he supposedly threw himself off his seventh floor apartment.

- Howard Carter opened the tomb on 16 February 1923, and died well over a decade later on 2 March 1939; however, some have still attributed his death to the "curse"

I wish to thank the people at http://apharaohs.blogspot.co.uk/ for their help in the research in this chapter.

ALCATRAZ

Alcatraz Island is situated just off of San Francisco Bay. It has a rich history and is best known for its time as a prison where it held some of America's most notorious and frightening criminals including Al Capone and Robert Franklin Stroud the "Bird Man of Alcatraz". The island is famous for its history of crime but it is also just as well known for its history of ghosts and hauntings.

Alcatraz Island belonged to Native Americans who owned the land and the earliest recorded owner was Julian Workman who bought it in 1846 with the understanding he would build and operate a light house on it. After this was fulfilled the island was sold to John C. Fermont of the Bear Flag Republic for $5000 so it could be used for military purposes. 1853 saw the first fortification of the Island and it was used for defence for the west of America.

During the American Civil War it was occupied by 200 soldiers and 11 cannons and the island was renamed Fortress Alcatraz. It was during this time that it was first used as a military prison. The first brick jail house was build in 1868 and between 1870 and 1876 a large modernisation was planned but was later scrapped for unknown reasons. The Island did continue as a long term detention centre.

The American-Spanish War of 1898 saw the prison grow from holding only 25-26 prisoners to over 450. A few years later the 1906 San Francisco Earthquake saw prisoners from all over California be transferred and held on Alcatraz while the other prisons were rebuilt or replaced. It was the following year which saw the Island become the official Western US Military

Prison.

As World War I took hold, Alcatraz became the holding place not just for prisoners but conscientious objectors – those who refused to perform military justice. One such CO was Philip Grosser who was held on the Island for refusing to fight during the war. He wrote a pamphlet about his experiences on Alcatraz entitled "Uncle Sam's Devil's Island". In it, he spoke of "Special Coffin Cages" and terrible isolation lasting "more that 23 hours a day".

The Military Prison was acquired by the US Department of Justice in 1933 who built the prison which still stands today. Alcatraz became a Federal Bureau Prison in August 1934 when the first 137 prisoners arrived on the Island.

During the following 29 years, Alcatraz held some of the most notorious criminals in American history including: Al Capone, Robert Franklin Stroud (the Birdman of Alcatraz), George "Machine Gun" Kelly, Bumpy Johnson, Rafael Cancel Miranda (a member of the Puerto Rican Nationalist

Party who attacked the United States Capitol building in 1954), Mickey Cohen, Arthur R. "Doc" Barker, James "Whitey" Bulger, and Alvin "Creepy" Karpis (who served more time at Alcatraz than any other inmate).

The Prison claimed that no prisoner ever escaped the island. The book and movie "Escape From Alcatraz" tells the true story of Frank Morris and the Anglin Brothers who attempted the most daring escape. Although no bodies were ever found, state officials have assumed they drowned. That said, there are many conspiracy theories out there as to their current whereabouts. Over all, 36 people tried to escape the prison. 23 were caught, 6 were shot and killed, two drowned and there were 5 missing, presumed dead. One such attempted escape resulted in the three day long Battle of Alcatraz where 3 people were killed and two were executed.

Due to high costs to keep the prison running, it was decided that Alcatraz would be closed in 1963. In 1964 a group of Native American Activists took over the island and soon after it became a National Historic Landmark. In 1986 it opened as a museum where numerous former guards and inmates returned to tell their stories.

Ever since the first people stood on Alcatraz ghosts have been sighed and experienced. Native Americans called it the "Evil Island" and refused to visit it. They also refused to grow crops on the land, believing that they too would become cursed. They would also report hearing strange "unnatural" noises coming from the island when they knew it was empty.

While it was used as a military base, people on the Island would report hearing phantom gun and cannon fire, possibly linked to its time during the Civil War and the author Mark Twain who once visited Alcatraz noted that "it is cold as winter even in the summer"

When Alcatraz became a working prison, both inmates and guards would report the ghostly goings-on in the building. Some would report seeing Native American Prison Guards who lost their lives in the

Civil War. While others would hear whispering, moaning, clanking chains and see floating blue lights in unoccupied cells. Most prisoners who reported such things would be declared insane and locked away in a cell known as "The Hole" which was in total isolation. One prisoner told guards that he could see floating red eyes in his cell. He was found dead the following day with "unidentified" purple marks on his neck.

Of course, the guards would laugh off such claims in front of the prisoners but would claim they experienced anomalies such as: hot and cold spots, unseen fingers on their necks, crying around the prison at night and fire alarms going off of their own accord with no real reason as to why. Some even reported seeing a phantom lighthouse on the island – this is still reported occasionally to this day.

Since closing as a prison and opening as a museum, visitors have now began to experience even more paranormal activity including: clanging sounds, crying, cell doors slamming shut, unexplained voices in cells 11 through 14D, the isolation cell "The

Hole" is noticeably colder than the rest of the building, sometimes 30 degrees colder even in the summer.

The famous inmates of Alcatraz are also experienced. The sound of a Banjo playing is heard coming from the shower block, this is where Al Capone would practice playing and his cell door is known to swing close. The Bird Man of Alcatraz is seen in his cell sitting on the bed with many canaries around him. George "Machine Gun" Kelly haunts the church while Alvin "Creepy" Karpis haunts the bakery and the kitchen.

The most haunted area of the Island is the now burned down Ward House. Prison guards, inmates and now tourists have all sighted a man with mutton chop style side burns, dressed as if he is going to a party. One guard once said he saw the man in the house and as he disappeared he made it so cold, the fire in the stove was extinguished.

Archaeologist findings have suggested that the site was once used as an Indian Burial Ground. Many classic horror films including

"Poltergeist", "The Amityville Horror" and "The Shining" all seem to have ghosts because their homes and hotels are on such a site. Could there be truth in this theory?

THE STANLEY HOTEL

The Stanley Hotel, situated in Estes Park, Colorado could arguably be the most known haunted location in the entire world due to being the hotel that inspired Stephen King to write his 1977 novel 'The Shining'.

It was built by Freelan Oscar Stanley, of the Stanley Steamer Fame which was an American Steam Engine Company, between 1903 and 1907. Freelan and his Wife Flora came to the Estes Park area in early 1903 to recovery from tuberculosis which they were both suffering from. As their health improved they decided to move permanently to the area and Freelan decided to build a hotel for others to come to and enjoy.

Freelan got his team together to build the hotel using rock and wood taken from the surrounding mountains and after four years of hard work, the hotel opened for business on July 4th, 1909.

The Stanley Hotel had all modern facilities including running water, electricity and telephones. There was no heating as it was intended to be a Summer Holiday resort rather than a winter resort.

It could be very easy to confuse the history of The Stanley Hotel and that of "The Overlook Hotel" which featured in Stephen King's The Shining or the popular 1980 Stanley Kubrick feature film of the same name. There is no evidence to suggest that the Stanley was built over an Ancient Indian Burial Ground, or that any murders took place there. That said, the Stanley Hotel does have an incredible reputation for being haunted.

As far back as the late 1920s staff at the hotel would report hearing a party going on in the Ball Room. They would go to check only to discover no party had taken place there. This continues to happen to this day. More recently staff and guests have reported hearing piano music playing from the Ball Room. One group of guests even reported seeing a lady who like Flora Stanley sitting playing the piano before disappearing.

In one of the guest bedrooms a man is often seen standing over the bed. Once the guest awakens and sees the man, he runs into the wardrobe slamming the door behind him. Upon inspection there is no one found in the wardrobe. He is said to be the same ghost who takes guest's watches, jewellery and luggage. People believe this to be the ghost of a guest at the hotel who took his own life in the 1940s.

Other ghosts reported at The Stanley Hotel include:

- Freelan and Flora seen dressed in formal clothing on the main staircase, lobby and the billiard room. Freelan is often seen in the administration office. Many believe he is there to keep an eye on the hotel's books.

- Disembodied voices and footsteps are heard in the hallways and in certain rooms, while unseen hands grab and pull at staff's clothes.

- In one bedroom, guests complain that they awake in the night to find their blankets have been removed from the bed and are folded nicely on the floor.

- The 4th Earl of Dunraven who previously owned the land before the Hotel was built is seen in room 407 where people often report smelling his cherry pipe tobacco. His face has also been seen at the window of the room when it is unoccupied.

- Room 418 is haunted by ghostly children who are heard running around the room and out in the hallway. They are sometimes seen playing with a ball.

- Most famously at the hotel is room 207. In 1911 there was a gas leak in the room which lead to an explosion which nearly killed the housekeeper, Elizabeth Wilson.

After the accident she was given a job at the hotel for life. After her death in the 1950s she has been seen in the room still keeping it clean after the explosion. Others have reported seeing dark figures in the room, something grabbing them by the throat and deep, dark threatening voices shouting at them from the darkness. Most frightening of all many people have reported seeing the imprint of a body lying on the bed which can quickly disappear.

In 1976, Stephen King and his wife were travelling in the area when their car broke down. They found the Stanley Hotel and begged the owner to allow them to stay the night. The hotel was just one day away from closing for the winter season. They were allowed to stay but were told that there was only the manager and two other members of staff there. That evening, King was on his way to his bedroom, Room 207, when he saw the ghost of a small child calling out for his nanny. The incident is what inspired King to write The Shining which was published a little over a year later.

The Stanley Hotel has another famous guest which has encountered the ghosts, the actor Jim Carrey. While filming the 1994 comedy feature "Dumb and Dumber" at the hotel, Carrey asked if he could spend a night in the infamous room 207. Once filming had finished for the day, Carrey retired to his room where only after a few hours did he flee the building, opting only to return to film scenes that couldn't be done in a studio. No one knows exactly what caused the actor to flee after such a short time, but some would argue he met The Stanley Hotel's ghostly guests.

It comes as no shock that the Hotel is often listed in countdowns of the world's most haunted properties. But with its rather happy history no one can be sure why the hotel is so haunted. Some suggest it could be to do with what happened on the land before. Others say the hotel could be cursed.

EDINBURGH VAULTS

The Edinburgh Vaults are a well known haunted site situated underground in Scotland's capital city, Edinburgh. The vaults are in fact a series of tunnels made up of the arches supporting the South Bridge. Building work was completed on the bridge and the vaults in 1788 and almost instantly began to be used as homes, businesses and pubs but slowly as time went on it became home to the underclass of Edinburgh and was a popular slum.

A generation of people were born in the vaults and lived their entire lives underground, never seeing daylight. It was a breeding ground for illness and disease with only a handful of doctors braving the conditions in the vaults to treat people. They would visit the vaults wearing Plague masks. (The masks look like duck beaks which is where the nickname for doctors, "Quacks" comes from). The poorest and worst off people seek refuge in the vaults while everyone else was leaving due to the damp. It would often flood in the vaults and over time people began to crowd into the same rooms to avoid the water. The vaults also became home to a number of people forced to move from their homes during the Highland Clearances.

The most famous occupants of the Vaults during this time were the notorious murderers and body snatchers Burke and Hare. The duo would snatch fresh corpses from the graveyard and store the bodies in the vaults until it was safe to move them to the surgery of Dr. Robert Knox for a price somewhere between £7.50 and £10.00. It is said that when the graveyards began to be watched by police, Burke and Hare had no choice but to turn to murder to deliver the corpses. They preyed on the unsuspecting people living in the vaults. They were eventually caught after delivering 16 bodied to Dr. Knox.

By 1820 the situation in the vaults had become so bad the decision was made to close the vaults all together. Many were warned that the vaults would be sealed up while other weren't. Many decided to stay where they had always lived - it was all they knew. The vaults were sealed up entirely by the end of 1825 with buckets of rubble used to conceal the entrances. No one can be sure of just how many people were still in the Vaults when it was sealed and any remaining people will have died a sad and lonely death down there.

It was over 100 years later that the Vaults were rediscovered, completely by accident when Scottish Rugby player, Norrie Rowan discovered a tunnel leading into them while helping a Romanian Rugby player seek political asylum weeks before the 1989 Romanian uprising. Norrie and his son Norman began a lengthy excavation of the vaults where they found human remains, toys, medicine bottles and other signs of human life.

Once the excavation work was completed it was decided that the Vaults should be open to the public to show how people lived down there. It wasn't long before people began to experience paranormal events down in the dark tunnels.

Almost from the start a series of violent hauntings occurred. People would see dark shadows, strange white mists floating along corridors and the feeling of being watched. Tour guides would hear their names being called out even though they were alone in the Vaults and tourists would feel an icy cold hand slowly move down their face.

The dark, nasty history of the vaults would account for the hauntings and a particular lady that is known to haunt the vaults has been picked up by a number of different mediums over the years. The lady in question is Mary McKinnon. Mary was the landlady of a tavern that was situated in the vaults in around 1822. One night a fight had broken out and keen to get the people that started it out of the pub, Mary grabbed a knife and began to threaten people. In the rush of everyone trying to leave, one man, who was a city clerk tripped up and fell on her knife and was killed. Mary was tried and found guilty of murder. She was hanged on April 16th 1822. Mary is said to still haunt the vaults trying to prove her innocence.

The most frightening haunting of the Vaults is that of a man known as "The Watcher". He is seen wandering the vaults and his only intent is to frighten people. He is noted as having a long ponytail and wears only black. Most worryingly of all, he has no face.

A woman dressed in red is seen who visibly shows off cuts to her throat and wrists. She was murdered along with two other woman in the vaults but only she is seen still hoping that her murderer will be caught and brought to justice.

Paranormal investigators who visit the vaults claim that batteries will drain moments after being replaced and that EMF Meters go off the scale. Incredible temperature fluctuations occur, sometimes with an amazing 15 degrees drop reported in just ten minutes.

In more recent times poltergeist activity has been reported in the Vaults. Paranormal Groups from around the country have had stones and bits of glass thrown at them and in some extreme cases investigators and members of the public have been cut and punched by unseen forces. Resulting in medical treatment in some of the most extreme cases.

Also in recent times, evidence of extreme torture in the vaults history have come to light as well as associations of witchcraft, both practice and trials. Could black magic be behind the vault's ghosts?

The sheer amount of activity has attracted tourists and ghost hunters from all around the country and the Vaults themselves have appeared on numerous radio and television programmes all over the world and there are hundreds of books out there filled with different accounts of hauntings.

The Edinburgh Vaults are definitely a "must see" location, but whatever you do, don't go alone because you never know what you are going to experience down there.

JAMES WARRENDER

WAVERLY HILLS SANATORIUM

Of all the guide books, lists, websites and television programmes based on the paranormal that are around, one location you can almost guarantee will appear within it is Waverly Hills Sanatorium. A location which has gained the title *the most haunted place in the world.* But what exactly has gained Waverly Hills that title?

Waverly Hills Sanatorium is a former tuberculosis hospital in Kentucky. It sits on land which was purchased by a Major Thomas S. Hays in 1883. Major Hays purchased the land as he needed room to build a school for his young daughter. Once he got the land he had a one roomed School House built and named it Waverly

Hills School – named after his love of Sir Walter Scott's Waverly novels.

In the early 20th Century, Jefferson County was stricken with an incredible outbreak of tuberculosis (or White Plague as it became known) so Major Hays sold the land to allow a two story tuberculosis hospital to be built on the site of the school. It was decided that it should retain the name of Waverly Hills. The original two story hospital, with enough room to treat 40 to 50 patients, opened on July 26, 1910.

As cases of tuberculosis worsened, the demand for the hospital meant that many people were missing out on the treatment they needed. An expansion in 1912 and a later expansion in 1924 meant the hospital could now hold over 400 patients, a capacity that was very quickly met.

At a time when medical knowledge wasn't as advanced as it is today, the hospital treated patients with heat lamps, fresh air, keeping the spirits high and constant reassurance of a full recovery, needless to say that these treatments weren't successful and attributed to the high death rate at the hospital.

Trying to keep the moral high in the hospital with the large amounts of deaths was difficult so it was decided that a tunnel would be built that descended 500 feet to the bottom of the hill so that the dead could be sneaked out of the building without the other patients from finding out.

The hospital continued to operate successfully until the early 1960s when medical science had developed enough and the antibiotic Streptomycin was introduced which lowered cases of tuberculosis dramatically. Such medical advancements meant hospitals such as Waverly Hills would become redundant. It finally closed in 1961 and was left abandoned. The building was purchased by Charlie and Tina Mattingly in 2001. They offer tours of the building focusing on its history and its ghosts.

No one can be entirely sure just how many people died in Waverly Hills. Some sources claim that there were as little as 152 a year while others suggest it could be as many as 63,000 in its relatively short time as a working hospital.

Since being abandoned Waverly Hills is said to be home to a number of ghosts, some good and worryingly, some bad. The most active area of the hospital is said to be the Tunnel – now nicknamed the "Death Tunnel" or "Body Chute". In this area many visitors have reported seeing dark shadows; both cold and hot spots and people have recorded some very sinister and threatening EVPs.

A young boy called Timmy is said to haunt the upper levels of the hospital. Many paranormal investigators have left balls for Timmy to play with in the area he haunts, only to come back later on and find that they have been moved, in some cases to entirely different parts of the building.

A murder or suicide is said to have taken place in Room 502. A nurse who found out she was pregnant by the owner of the hospital. She either killed herself, or was murdered by the owner on finding out the news. Her spirit is often seen in room 502 or walking around the corridors.

Else where, other dark figures have been witnessed wondering about the hallways and some of the wards. Different coloured wisps of white or dark coloured mist have been captured on camera or witnessed with the naked eye. Investigators report a high level of success while using thermal imaging cameras, some capturing full figures with them. Most worryingly of all, in the last few years at the hospital, investigators and the occasional tourist have been cut by an unseen force, mainly in the morgue area.

It is now very clear to see why the building has received the title as *the most haunted place in the world.* Not just because of its history but because of the very different spirits that haunt the hospital and as it seems not all are good and not all know that they have passed on.

CONCLUSION

You have researched the end of this particular volume of my paranormal research. I hope you have enjoyed it and I really do hope you have taken away some knowledge that will help you and your own paranormal investigations.

Please check out my website, the address can be found at the start of the book and feel free to get in contact about what you have read or for any more help or information.

I do hope no one will have sleepless nights after reading my work but in the mean time do remember that no matter where you are, the 'Angels of the Odd' are watching you.

All the best,

James

- 2014

ABOUT THE AUTHOR

James Warrender was born in Aberdeen in 1991. He began studying the paranormal in 2003 and moved into investigation in 2005. He has appeared in television, radio and print discussing the subject.

Outside the paranormal world, Warrender lectures and writes.

Angels of the Odd is Warrender's first book.

Made in the USA
Middletown, DE
25 November 2024